# THE *Just* AND THE *Unjust Alike*

Volume 2 in
*The Last Rose of Autumn Collection*

*Nine short stories about making wrong things right*

BY DEBBIE WELLS NOBIS

xulon PRESS

Copyright © 2014 by Debbie Wells Nobis

The Just and the Unjust Alike
Volume 2 in: The Last Rose of Autumn Collection
by Debbie Wells Nobis

Printed in the United States of America

ISBN 9781498401210

All rights reserved solely by the author. The author guarantees all contents are original and do not infringe upon the legal rights of any other person or work. No part of this book may be reproduced in any form without the permission of the author. The views expressed in this book are not necessarily those of the publisher.

All names of people, businesses, and places, etc. are fictional, and any similarity to real people, businesses, or places, etc. is purely coincidental.

Scripture quotations taken from the New King James Version (NKJV). Copyright © 1979, 1980, 1982 by Thomas Nelson, Inc. Used by permission. All rights reserved.

Scripture quotations taken from the King James Version (KJV) – public domain

www.xulonpress.com

# TABLE OF CONTENTS

*Foreword*............................ vii

Duty......................................9
Mrs. Murphy and the Mob ................37
Bubba's Girl ............................50
Not Yet ................................57
Somebody's Daddy ......................76
Calliope Jane............................86
Harvest Gold and Avocado Green............95
The Ghost of Jerry Paganelli................99
Extenuating Circumstances.................120

*Bible References* ........................125

# FOREWORD

I have way too many stories for one book, so this is Volume 2, in the Last Rose of Autumn Collection. God gave me the title, *The Just and the Unjust Alike*, saying that He sends the rain on the just and the unjust (Matthew 5:45 NKJV), and that He sent Jesus, the just for the unjust (1 Peter 3:18 NKJV). I've heard these scriptures all my life, but when I searched for the exact references, "alike" isn't in these verses; and I prayed about dropping alike from the title.

However, God said "I chose *alike* because I love you all the same." John 3:16 NKJV says: "For God so loved the world that He gave His only begotten Son, that whoever believes in Him should not perish but have everlasting life." *Whoever!* Just or unjust, God loves us all.

# DUTY

❦

Clutch in, shift, clutch out, gas. Clutch in, shift, clutch out, gas. Hill: clutch in, downshift, brake. No! Gas, clutch out, shift. GRIND! Too many hills! There were too many hills for a road that led to a place called The Flats.

Frustrated but undeterred, Mrs. Evelyn Anders struggled with the gears and the hills, and drove on. The day before, the County Sheriff had called with news that Mrs. Marcella Brown, the Anders' former housekeeper had had a stroke or something and could use some help. Unsympathetic and uninterested in the poor woman's plight, he had directed Mrs. Anders to send the Brown woman some money and wash her hands of the situation. His instructions were immediately disregarded.

Yes, they lived in troubled times. 1963 was a tumultuous year, and Mrs. Anders knew that calling a colored servant, friend, was dangerous, so she kept her thoughts to herself, but her feelings for Marcie Brown ran deep. They had met as young women and grown old together. Marcie had stayed by her side through many dark days in the Anders' household, and now that she was in need, her Miss Evvie would not abandon the devoted housekeeper.

She informed the Sheriff that she would go see Mrs. Brown, and decide for herself what was best.

Annoyed, Sheriff Jess had repeated his advice against going to The Flats, adding that Mrs. Brown's problems weren't Miss Evvie's business anymore. A widow herself, Mrs. Anders had inarguably replied that it was her duty as a Christian to attend to widows and orphans. Fed up with the conversation, the Sheriff had given a vague reply about having fulfilled *his* duty and ended the call before his constituent could ask him to accompany her.

She had thought of insisting that he escort her, but knew he would comply with ill grace and elected to go alone. *"Greater is He who is in me, than he who is in the world,"* she thought. After all, the location may be awful, but the people weren't.

The Flats wasn't much, just a cluster of forlorn shanties huddled on the hills near the river bottom. It was where poor colored people went to live, when they were flat broke. Marcie and her husband had moved there three years earlier, when Mr. Brown had become too ill to continue working at the sawmill.

At the time, Miss Evvie had openly expressed concern for the Brown's and offered to help. Although truly grateful, Marcie had declined, explaining that she and Sam would not accept charity. Samuel

Brown was a good man, and Miss Evvie did not fault him for his pride, she simply wished things were different. You see, no bus service ran between The Flats and the town, Marcie would have to retire also. It wasn't what she was used to, but Marcie knew she could cope with the inconveniences of The Flats, parting ways with Miss Evvie would be her biggest trial. With a heavy heart, she had packed the pictures, letters, and knick-knacks she referred to as her Remembrances, and gone to make the best of a sour situation

As Marcie's ramshackle cabin came into sight, the car began to lurch. Exasperated, Miss Evvie pushed in the clutch and coasted to the bottom of the hill. When she let out the clutch, the car bucked and died. The weary driver let the car roll to the side of the road near the path to Marcie's cabin then heaved a sigh of relief, shifted into what she hoped was first gear, and set the hand brake. She straightened her hat then took the key out of the ignition, diligently placing it on top of the sun visor. Turning the car around would have to wait; right now, she was anxious to get to her friend.

Unsure what she would find, the visitor gingerly trod up the pieces of slab wood laid in a steep path to the cabin. Bright green tufts of grass grew between the warped boards, but they still rocked, and Miss Evvie found it difficult to keep her balance. The last slab wobbled so much that she grabbed the hand rail on the porch steps to steady herself. The rotted lumber gave way, and the rail swayed wildly.

"My heavens!" The porch was in imminent danger of collapsing, and she prayed that the steps wouldn't buckle under her weight. The sooner she got Marcie out of this place, the better.

Her plan was simple: she was going to convince her former housekeeper to come back and be her live-in companion. It might take some persuasive talking, Marcie was a proud, independent woman, but it sounded feasible. That is it had until the last big step required to get onto the porch made Miss Evvie wonder if she had bitten off more than she could chew. If Marcie *had* suffered a stroke, how would she get down to the car? Fear spurred Miss Evvie's imagination, and her concerns multiplied like warm Coca Cola foaming out of a shaken bottle on a hot day.

Then she knocked on the door and heard Marcie's slurred voice fretfully asking who was there. All doubts were set to flight, and Miss Evvie's strength soared.

"Marcie, it's Miss Evvie, Marcie!" She pulled on the screen door but it wouldn't budge. She could see Marcie struggling to raise herself from an old sofa in the middle of the room, and the determined little visitor punched her gloved hand through the rusted screen and flipped the hook holding the door.

Marcie laughed and cried as she held out her right hand in welcome. "What you doin' here, chil'?

This ain' no place for you. Oh, but I shorly am glad to see you! Did Mr. Jess come wif you? Never tell me you come here by yoself. Wha'm I gonna do wif you?" she scolded without heat. "You as white as a sheet, chil'. You been drivin' that awful ol' car of Mr. John's, ain' you?"

"Well, I heard that you died, so I came to see for myself." It was an old joke between them. There were so many Browns that it was a challenge to keep them all straight.

"Died? I don' think so! Come and sit a spell, res' yoself."

The cabin was filthy. Dirt crunched under Miss Evvie's feet, and sluggish dust bunnies lolled back and forth, snared on the rough floor boards. The scant furniture was arranged awkwardly, probably so Marcie could steady herself on it; and worn out lace curtains hanging at the dingy windows did little to keep out the glaring sunlight. A chipped cup sat on a broken chair beside the sofa, and crocks and pans rested upside down on the kitchen table, imperfectly covering the piles they were intended to protect.

The room looked depressing and smelled like a chamber pot that needed emptied, none of which mattered to Miss Evvie as she pulled off her gloves and tucked her hand under Marcie's ankles swinging her legs off of the sofa to help the invalid sit up. The thoughtful guest sat down on a lumpy cushion and locked her hand onto Marcie's as it groped for hers.

"Wha'm I gonna do wif you?" Marcie repeated then paused. "I'm so embarrassed. You shouldn' be seein' me in all this dirt."

"Goose, I didn't come to inspect your house. I came to see you, and you're not well. What's wrong."

"I thinks I done had me a stroke. My lef' side don' work so good, an' I cain' get up an' down them steps hardly t'all. It's mighty tiresome some days, mighty tiresome, but the good Lord, He strengthens me. Yes, He does," and she squeezed Miss Evvie's hand reassuringly.

"I know He's your rock, but, Marcie, you can't stay here. I won't have it. I don't see a picture or a knick-knack anywhere. And if you tell me those wash tubs and bowls are turned upside down on the table because you like it that way, you may think again, missy. Does the roof leak?"

"Like a sieve!"

"Then the landlord must fix it!"

"He ain' gonna fix nothin'," Marcie grieved shaking her head dolefully. "An' I gots to leave here anyways. I ain' had the money to pay the rent for some time now, an' Mr. Tobias done tol' the Sheriff to put me out." So that was why Sheriff Jess had called.

The note of resignation in Marcie's voice did not deceive Miss Evvie. She tightened her grip on the hand in her lap and silently asked for God's help. "Where will you go?"

"I don' know wha' I'm a gonna do. Oh Miss Evvie," she whispered brokenly, "I think they gonna send me to the Poor Farm."

The very words evoked horror, and Miss Evvie recoiled at the thought. The Poor Farm was nothing more than a disgusting kennel filled with abandoned souls waiting to die. Marcie could not go there. "No, I won't have it," she stated unequivocally. "I came here intending to persuade you to come live with me, and that's what I'm going to do. You may consider the issue settled. We may have to crawl off those steps and roll down the hill, but I am *not* leaving here without you."

Before Marcie could reply, the screen door screeched, loudly yielding as a strong hand forced it back on its rusty hinges, and a man the size of a bear blocked the doorway. "Not meanin' any offense, ma'am, but who is you, and what's ya'll's business with Miz Brown here?" the man demanded.

"Oh, I'm so glad you've come!" exclaimed Miss Evvie jumping up. Taken by surprise, the man stared. It wasn't her 5'1" that disarmed him, it was her smile. "I'm Mrs. John Anders," she continued, "Mrs. Brown used to be my housekeeper. Now that Mr. Brown has passed, I've asked her to come back to me, but I need help getting her to the car."

"Ma'am, what kind a work does y'all think a po' ol' crippled lady gonna do?" he wondered.

"It's my doilies," improvised Miss Evvie. "Nobody does them up the way Miss Marcie did.

## The Just and the Unjust Alike

She can train the new help and watch over them. And you know I can't be driving back and forth to fetch her, so she'll have to live-in."

Marcie had taken hold of Miss Evvie's hand, and the man studied the two elderly women for a moment before dryly advising: "Y'all best come up with a better story than that before yous runs into that wicked, mean sheriff. He don' hold with white folk mixin' with coloreds."

The ladies smiled at him, and Marcie purred: "Thank you, Norvelle Clay."

He threw up his hands. "I *knows* when I'm whipped. Iffin' you was to give me the keys to your car, ma'am, I'd turn it round so yous can get in easy-like. And I'll carry out Miz Brown's things, and he'p y'all down them steps."

"The key is on the sun visor," answered Miss Evvie.

The man gave her an avuncular scowl. "Y'all ought'n to do that in a place like this, ma'am." And as he went out to move the car, he grumbled under his breath the way men do sometimes.

"I cain' go to town, lookin' like this," protested Marcie fumbling with a broken button on the tattered shirt she wore over her dress. "My clothes is all dirty, and I looks me a fright."

"Well I'm not driving back to this place, Marcie Brown, and I won't leave you behind, so pull up your socks and put on your hat because we're not staying here!"

Marcie chuckled and tugged at the elastic garters rolled up in her stockings. "You always was a feisty little thing. I s'pose you gonna have yo way, so I may's well spare me my breath."

"That's the most sensible thing you've said since I got here," agreed Miss Evvie. "Where's your hat?"

A short time later, Marcie's meager possessions were stowed in the trunk of the car, and she was taking one last look around. "I jus wanna make sure we done got all my Remembrances," she explained. "They ain' much, but they's precious to me. Pictures and letters is all I got lef' to me now," she sighed.

Miss Evvie knew the lonely widow was thinking of her daughter, Janna, the Brown's only child to have survived the influenza epidemic some 30 years earlier. Beautiful and smart, the talented young woman had married a nice man and gone to live in Chicago. She was the light of her mother's life, and when Janna had stopped writing, Marcie's world had gone gray.

Miss Evvie nodded understandingly as she picked up her dear friend's handbag and Bible, and turned her toward the door. "Got your teeth?" she asked, and Marcie patted the handbag.

Outside, Norvelle Clay helped the ladies down the hill and waited patiently beside the car while Marcie got situated. He then instructed Miss Evvie to get in beside her, firmly stating his intention to drive the ladies out to the hard road. The spunky little widow yearned to defend her driving skills, but was so relieved that she humbly thanked him instead, and got in beside Marcie without arguing.

"He must'a see'd you drive in, chil'," remarked her Job's Comforter knowingly.

A few miles from town, Mr. Clay found a place to stop, and opened the back door for Miss Evvie. She offered to pay the Good Samaritan, but he refused explaining that it was his duty as a Believer to help those he could. "Iff'n you don't mind though, ma'am, I'd take it mighty kindly iff'n you ladies was to pray for me."

"Ain' no time like the present," quipped Marcie, and the man took off his hat and knelt in the grass close to the car. "Matthew 5:16 says: *Let yo' light shine before men, that they may see yo' good works and glorify yo' Father in Heaven.* And I speaks that ov'a yo' life, Norvelle Clay. In Jesus' name, yo' light gonna shine, son. Amen!"

He felt a another hand rest on the opposite shoulder, and a strange energy moved across his back between the two. His head swam a little, and the large man felt the presence of God in way he had not known before. He thought Mrs Brown would lay her hand on him, he had not expected Mrs Anders to do the same, and was even more shocked that she had taken off her glove. Only God could move folks this way, he thought.

"Proverbs 3:5-6 says '*Trust in the Lord with all thine heart, and lean not unto thine own understanding; in all thy ways acknowledge Him, and He shall direct thy paths.*' I speak that over you and yours Mr. Clay, that God the Father will guide your paths." said Miss Evvie blessing him. "In Jesus' name, amen."

He thanked the ladies then held the driver's door for Miss Evvie, and sent them on their way with a wave of his hat as he chuckled: "Damn fool Sheriff best not tangle with them two, no sir!"

There were a few more hills to negotiate before they reached the Anders' house, but Marcie knew how difficult it was to handle Mr. John's car and encouraged the nervous driver with gentle words of praise and confident assurances that Mr. Cody down to the garage would be able to repair any damage to the transmission.

When the car finally pulled into the carriage drive and stopped beside the French doors, both ladies were immensely relieved to be back at the large brick house. The night before, Miss Evvie had made up the studio couch in what used to be Mr. John's reading room. It was on the main floor, and Marcie would not have to climb the stairs to the servants' quarters. Marcie was deeply touched by the thoughtfulness, but declared that she was too dirty to lay down on the fresh bedding and instructed Miss Evvie to spread out an old blanket for her to rest on. As soon as she was settled, her hostess went to her own room and fell asleep.

The sun had gone down when Miss Evvie woke up. She checked on Marcie who was still sleeping, and left her new housemate to rest while she went out back and prepared the wash house. When she returned, Marcie called to her saying that if Miss Evvie would help her up, she'd fix some supper. Even though she hated to cook, Miss Evvie replied: "We'll have scrambled eggs and toast, I'll fix it. Do you want to eat first or clean up?" she asked handing Marcie a glass of fresh tea. Marcie wanted to wash, but firmly stated that no matter how badly she wanted a bath, she was not going to the second floor in the dumbwaiter. Miss Evvie laughed, she hadn't thought of that. Instead, she helped Marcie to the French doors where an old red wagon that once belonged to the Anders' son was parked. Marcie's owlish look made her helper laugh again, and she explained her plan to roll Marcie around to the wash house where two kettles of hot water were ready to use.

Always game, Marcie eased herself onto the folded comforter Miss Evvie had laid in the wagon, and held up her lame leg by tucking her right ankle under it and lifting as they began to move. The cobblestone sidewalk made for a jolting ride, and Marcie regaled the short trip by singing a choppy hymn. Miss Evvie smiled. It was like old times.

In the wash house, Miss Evvie helped Marcie out of her clothes covertly noticing that the bather's left hand did not function well enough to maneuver buttons. That was probably why Marcie wore her husband's shirt over her dress. Without the layers of clothes, Marcie looked very thin. Distressed at her emaciated condition but trying to be light-hearted, Miss Evvie exclaimed: "Marcie, what happened to your bosoms? They look like a pair of fried banty eggs."

"Humph, I don' know what you be squawkin' 'bout, girl. Dem things hangin' off you looks like a pair a ol' socks wif mashed taters in the toe."

"They do not!" denied Miss Evvie until she leaned over and caught a glimpse down her own cleavage. She burst out laughing and had to grab her mouth to keep her false teeth in place. "Well, we used to be young and beautiful, didn't we?"

"Don' fret yoself, chil', we still the bes' lookin' women in this here wash house," observed Marcie with spirit.

They sat at the black and white enamel kitchen table to have their supper, and Marcie asked why the room had not been painted recently. "Every five years, tha's when yous painted. I makes it five years las' year. You cain' be letting' yo house fall to ruin jus' cause you gettin' on in years," she lectured kindly.

Miss Evvie looked around and acknowledged that she hadn't noticed how tired the room had become. "It always mattered more to you than it did to me," she remarked honestly. "Tomorrow, I'll get some fabric swatches for new curtains and pick up some paint chips. What color do you have in mind?

Oh dear, I'd better start a list or I'll forget half of what you tell me."

The next morning, Miss Evvie set out right after breakfast. She wanted to talk with a specific painter, and the most likely place to run him to ground at this hour was at Carter's Hardware picking up supplies. She had just finished gathering a selection of paint chips when Mr. Joshua Washington and his daughter, Etta, came in the side door. He greeted Mrs. Anders, and she told him about wanting to have her kitchen painted, and added that she had also decided to change the wallpaper in Mr. John's reading room.

"I don't know the paint color yet," she said, "but assuming there's enough of it, that pink paper in the returned goods will do nicely for the reading room. When might you be able to start?" Mr. Washington said he would need to look at his book, and offered to meet her at her car, if she didn't mind waiting a minute.

Armed with his calendar, the man apologized explaining that it would be several weeks before he personally could get to her job. However, if she didn't mind, his son was home from school, and he and another young fellow would be able to start right away. She agreed stating that she knew he would not make the offer unless the young men were competent. She would also need them to move some furniture because Miss Marcie was with her again, and Miss Evvie wished for her to sleep in the reading room.

As their client drove away, his daughter's resentment boiled over. "She wants a room for her maid," Etta mocked, "so she picks leftover wallpaper that somebody else didn't want to refurbish it. That makes me sick."

"Hold your tongue, child. I've worked for Miss Evvie nigh on 25 years, she picks greens and blues to please herself. Pink is Miss Marcie's favorite color. I don't know what work she's fit for, but Miss Marcie is too old a woman to be climbing three flights of stairs to sleep in the attic. Fixin' a room for her on the first floor, that's pure kindness. And that wallpaper you're so peevish about is them bolts from Italy the banker's wife turned up her nose at. It's the highest priced wallpaper in the whole store, and we're gonna hang it in the housekeeper's room," he chortled.

Miss Evvie's next stop was Melton's Fabrics where she picked up some swatches for the curtains. She also made a number of purchases predicted to make Marcie as mad as a wet hen, and arranged for a seamstress to come to the house the following day to take measurements. After that, Miss Evvie walked around the corner of the square to Rexalls where she purchased Cameo soap and Ponds Cold Cream for Marcie's dry skin. She was pondering over the forth thing on her list when the answer spoke her name. She wanted to see a doctor about Marcie and would not have thought of consulting Dr. David Feinman, but he was right in front of her, so Miss Evvie took it as a sign from God.

David had grown up with the Anders' son, and Miss Evvie knew she could rely on him. Well aware of prying ears, she paid her bill, and asked David to carry her package to the car. None of the onlookers seemed to think it odd for a doctor to carry her package, not a Jewish doctor anyway.

Outside, she asked about David's family, and they discussed every day matters until she mentioned that Miss Marcie was with her again. He was glad for both their sakes and told her so. He hadn't seen Miss Marcie for a long time and asked about her health. His old neighbor pressed her lips together to keep from pouring out her heart within earshot of the men sitting on the park bench near her car. Instead, she answered him with a question: "David, if I need you, would you come to the house?"

"Of course," he replied discreetly writing his phone numbers on the brown paper bag holding her purchases. David's mother had passed away when he was 13, and Miss Evvie and Miss Marcie had comforted and nurtured the shy boy any way they could. He would always think of them fondly.

Krogers was the last stop on the list, and planning meals for two made grocery shopping feel like a holiday. With her most pressing concern addressed, Miss Evvie would have enjoyed herself very much, if only she had not encountered Mrs. Gloriosa Tharpe.

"Miss Evelyn," barked the bossy socialite without preamble, "what's this I hear about you taking that Marcella Brown creature into your house? *Marcella*? That's a mighty uppity name for a maid."

"Good day, Miss Gloriosa, how are you?" replied her prey with exacting politeness. "It always amazes me how you are so quick to gather the news."

"Well, I do pride myself on keeping abreast," preened the haughty gossip. "However, you did *not* answer me."

Thinking that it was none of her darn business, Miss Evvie refused to take the bait, and eluded the intent of the question with: "Mrs. Brown *has* been kind enough to return to me."

"Merciful heavens, one must have help, but *must* you have that Nigra living under the same roof?"

Miss Evvie's eyes flashed dangerously. She realized that Mrs. Tharpe knew very little about mercy or heaven to talk the way she did, but she still itched to give the mouthy bigot a crisp piece of her mind. It took a great deal of patience to rely on Proverbs 15:1 and remember that *a soft word turns away wrath*. "I'm not a young woman," Miss Evvie explained, "and I don't have the energy to train an endless stream of servants the way you do, Miss Gloriosa. When you get to be my age, you're grateful when someone who already knows your ways is willing to put up with you."

Dissatisfied but stumped for a reply, Mrs. Tharpe left, and Miss Evvie returned to her shopping. That evening, Marcie delightedly helped fix a lovely supper, although she ate less than Miss Evvie would have liked.

Come morning, the house bustled with people. Mr. Washington's son, Caleb, and his friend, Will, unloaded tools and ladders and began stripping wallpaper in the reading room. A little later, Miss Tammy, the seamstress from Meltons, arrived to measure the kitchen windows...and Miss Marcie. The windows were no challenge, Miss Marcie proved less cooperative. Proclaiming that new dresses were quite unnecessary, she stubbornly refused to cooperate until Miss Evvie was called out of the room to answer questions for the men, and Miss Tammy could do what she did best, negotiate.

The soft-spoken little woman was not the most skilled seamstress at Meltons, she was, however, the wisest, and thoughtfully remarked that while dressing in worn out clothes might be a noble gesture, it would cast Miss Evvie in an unflattering light. People would say she was cheap. Most employers provided uniforms for their help, and if Miss Evvie wished for Miss Marcie to wear house dresses instead of uniforms, well, wasn't that her prerogative?

Fiercely protective, Marcie tartly advised Miss Tammy to take up politics, and grudgingly allowed herself to be measured. Miss Evvie, who knew more about clothes than curtains, showed Miss Tammy the trims she had purchased for each of the dresses and explained that they must open all the way down the front and button to the right so Miss Marcie could dress more conveniently.

Their momentary rift mended, Miss Evvie and Marcie prepared a wonderful lunch and gave the young men plates that they carried to a shade tree in the back yard. Modern folks didn't feed workers anymore, but Miss Evvie didn't aspire to be modern. She appreciated the young men and wished to bless their efforts. She also needed advice from them. After two days with Marcie, Miss Evvie had admitted to herself that they really did need to hire some help, and she asked Caleb and Will if they knew one, no, two young women who were available to do the cleaning and some cooking. They said yes, and Marcie started a chore list.

Etta and a quiet girl, named Rhinnie, came with the men the following day. Marcie was still in bed. She hadn't slept well, and didn't have the energy to get up. Not wishing to disturb her but needing to move the studio couch and its occupant to another room, Caleb and Will picked up the couch, with her on it, and carried the whole lot to the music room where Miss Evvie was setting up a temporary bedroom. Marcie laughed and announced that she felt like Cleopatra.

By noon, Cleopatra felt more like a sick cat than a queen. Miss Evvie would have called for a doctor right then, only Marcie wouldn't allow it. Her back ached, and she was over taxed from the excitement of moving; she just needed to rest a spell. As proof, she spent the day sleeping on and off, and eating very little.

Nightfall came, and the pain in Marcie's back worsened. Miss Evvie asked if she felt feverish. Marcie flatly denied it, joking that the only thermometer in the house was the candy thermometer, and they already knew she was hardboiled, so why make a fuss.

Around midnight, the fever was undeniable. Miss Evvie sat beside her friend putting cold washcloths on her forehead and wiping her arms and legs with vinegar water in an effort to make her more comfortable. Nothing helped. By 4:00 a.m., Miss Evvie was deeply worried and got out Dr. Feinman's home phone number, forcing herself to wait until 5:00 to call. He answered on the second ring.

"David, it's Miss Evvie," she said. "I'm so sorry to bother you, dear. Can you come over right away?" She did not say why in case the local switchboard operator was eavesdropping. In turn, Dr. Feinman simply replied that he would be there in 15 minutes.

Miss Evvie was watching and opened the door before he could knock. "It's Miss Marcie. I think she has kidney infection. Her back hurts, and she's feverish," she explained motioning toward the music room and hurrying to keep up with him. Dr. Feinman set his bag down on the floor beside the studio couch and knelt down to examine Marcie.

"Hello there, Miss Marcie," he greeted with a coaxing smile. "What have you gotten in to?"

"Is tha you Mr. Davy?" she asked clutching his hand. "Now I knows I be in trouble, chil'. Ain' you the doctor for dead folks?"

"Yes," he chuckled, "I'm the coroner, but I am a real doctor."

"Iffin' you says so, chil'," she acquiesced skeptically allowing him to take her temperature and blood pressure. After that, he listened to her heart and slid his hands under her back pressing against her kidneys. Marcie moaned: "Please don' do that no more, Mr. Davy. You be hurtin' me somethin' fearful!"

"I'm sorry to hurt you, but I agree with Miss Evvie. I think you have a urinary tract infection. Is there a sample I can take to the lab?" Miss Evvie lifted the towel covering the pot Marcie had been using, and Dr. Feinman nodded. "I'm going to leave some medicine for you to start on, and after I run a couple of tests, I'll have the pharmacy bring over something more, if you need it Take one of these every 4 hours with a little food, and Miss Marcie, I want you to drink a jelly glass full of water every hour."

"Tha's not convenient," argued his patient. Miss Evvie knew she meant that it was not convenient to get up to use the pot, and smoothed over the disagreement by assuring him that they would manage.

After the doctor left, Marcie swallowed a pill but attempted to decline most of the water. Miss Evvie refused to back down, and the cantankerous invalid drank half the glass promising to take care of the rest in a minute. When Miss Evvie went to the kitchen to make her a piece of toast, Marcie reached for the glass and tossed what was left in it out the window.

Miss Evvie accurately suspected that Marcie's illness was just starting. In spite of the medication, her fever mounted, and she thrashed, fitfully trying to find a more comfortable position. As the hours wore on, she hallucinated, and bad dreams about not being able to reach her daughter tormented her. Why hadn't Janna written? Why had her mother's letters been returned? Had she and her family been swept up in the race riots? Was she angry? Her letters stopped shortly after Mr. Brown's death, did Janna think her mother had failed him?

Then Marcie's mind would drift to her three children who had died in the influenza epidemic, and she would sob uncontrollably with Miss Evvie weeping helplessly beside her.

As nursing took more and more of her time, Miss Evvie depended on Etta to do the cooking and answer Caleb's questions. "Do as you think best," deferred Miss Evvie, and Etta took the reins. She was a very astute young woman, and it didn't escape her notice that no matter how much Miss Evvie asked the young women to do, she never asked them to empty the pot or wash soiled bedding. And when Marcie became too weak to get up, it was Miss Evvie who washed the diapers made from pieces of an old flannel blanket. Etta didn't understand. Most folks delegated the worst chores first. She wasn't complaining, mind you, she just didn't understand.

It was a struggle, but tribulations don't last forever, and by the forth day, Marcie was in her right mind, even though she was very weak. The grandfather clock in the foyer struck 11:00 p.m., and Miss Evvie came in with fresh water. She put a straw in the glass and held it for Marcie to drink.

"I don' wan' it!" complained the testy patient, pushing the glass away.

Miss Evvie set the glass down with a bang and plunked herself on the chair beside to the studio couch. "Then I suppose I'll just have to sit here and wait until you are ready, missy." Concerned and exhausted, the muscles in Miss Evvie's jaws worked as she bit back strong words. She was dreadfully worried that Marcie had given up, and was ready to die. She may not have seen her old friend much in the past three years, but knowing that they were only a few miles apart had given Miss Evvie comfort.

She sat fuming over Marcie's refusal to help herself, until memories of an earlier time, a time when *she* had been in bed, and Marcie had been on the chair, came to her mind, and Miss Evvie started to cry. An unsteady mahogany hand reached out and took hold of hers.

"I reckon I be havin' me som' a tha' water now, iffin' you was still of a mind to hep me wif it," whispered Marcie repentantly.

"Oh Marcie, how did you stand me? I was so terrible!"

Marcie remembered: "How was I gonna be mad at you, chil'? There you was, wif that awful telegram sayin' Mr. Jack done give his life fo' the war. Yo heart broke clean to pieces, and di'n I know it. We gonna be awright. We been through too much to give up now, chil'." Marcie drank the water, they prayed, and Miss Evvie laid down on a sofa near her. The two friends slept through till morning.

The smell of coffee wafting through the house woke Miss Evvie who stretched and reached for the pail she kept Marcie's diapers in; it was empty, and the pot had been emptied and washed. She went to look for the girls and saw the missing diapers swinging from the clothesline.

"Oh, Etta, I didn't intend for you to wash those things," she apologized.

"I know, but you told me to do what I thought was best, ma'am, and that's what I did. Now, tell me what you want for your breakfast."

Miss Evvie sat down to enjoy her coffee, and the girls continued their conversation.

"Was it Mrs. Jonas Brown or Mrs. Joshua Brown who died? I can never keep those two straight. My auntie married a man named Jacob Brown, but everyone calls him Bunny," said Rhinnie.

Etta's reply would have to wait. "Rhinnie, how do you get a phone number for someone in another city?" interrupted Miss Evvie.

"Well, they have phone books for nearly every city at the public library, but they're pretty old. For a newer number, the best thing would be to call information, if you don't mind the cost."

"I don't care how much it costs, that's what I want you to do, today, please. Get the number for Edwin K. Jones in Chicago. The last address I have for him is on Vine Street. If that doesn't work, call every Edwin Jones in the Chicago area. And don't tell Miss Marcie, use the phone upstairs, please."

"Of course, Miss Evvie, but what's this about, if you don't mind me asking, ma'am?"

"I think we need to bring Miss Marcie back from the dead," she replied mysteriously. The young women traded wide-eyed stares, and their employer laughed and explained about Miss Marcie losing contact with her daughter.

The number for Edwin K. Jones on Vine Street had been disconnected, and even though there were an amazing number of Edwin Jones's listed in the Chicago area, Rhinnie had no luck finding the right one until late in the afternoon. Her mouth was dry, and her head ached when she called the next to the last number on her list. A pleasant lady answered, and Rhinnie hoarsely repeated her little speech. "Hello, I'm looking for Mrs. Janna Jones, her husband's name is Edwin. Do I have the right number?"

"No, dear, I'm sorry, that Edwin is my husband's nephew. He and Janna moved to Peoria about a year ago."

"Oh my God, oh my God, oh my God!" jabbered Rhinnie dancing down the stairs. "Miss Evvie, Miss

Evvie come quick, I have the number you asked me to get!"

Wanting to spare Marcie as much pain as possible, Miss Evvie went upstairs to call to Peoria. It was as she suspected, Janna had been given wrong information. Mail service to The Flats was sporadic and unreliable, so when her letters to her mother had been returned, Janna had called the Sheriff's office and mistakenly been told that her mother was dead and buried.

Her heart broke all over again when she heard the truth, and Edwin had to take over the conversation. Miss Evvie considerately told him that she would tell Marcie then call back. Marcie cried too, but she shed happy tears and quickly pulled herself together begging Miss Evvie to call and not waste any more precious time. The reunited mother and daughter talked for more than an hour.

Miss Evvie invited the Jones's to come visit and plans were made; but in the mean time, the ladies were expecting other guests. Brother Orrin from the First Baptist Church was coming to visit Miss Marcie, and Mrs. Gloriosa Tharpe had invited herself to tea with Miss Evvie. Less than delighted but none-the-less gracious, her hostess went to the kitchen to check on the tea trays and noticed a mix up. She had placed two tins of cookies on the kitchen table, and Etta had put the freshly baked cookies on the delicate china plate for Miss Evvie's guest and yesterday's cookies on the plate for Miss Marcie's guest.

"You have that backwards, dear," she told Etta kindly. "Just pick up the doilies, and I'll switch the plates."

Etta stared at her confusing employer for a moment, then pressed her fists into her hips and exclaimed: "Miss Evvie, sometimes, I don't understand you at all."

Miss Evvie smiled knowingly. "Etta, the world is full of bumptious people, and the sooner you learn to deal with them the better. Gloriosa Tharpe is wealthy, influential, and as toxic as the flower she's named after. I have to put up with her, I don't have to reward her with Miss Marcie's secret recipe cookies. Miss Gloriosa is a trial, but she keeps putting herself in my presence, so I remind myself that it's my Christian Duty to show her God's love, and pray that someday, some of it will soak in."

Etta glanced out the kitchen window and saw Marcie sitting in the shade. "I suppose taking care of Miss Marcie is a duty too," sighed the young woman.

Laughter rolled out of Miss Evvie causing the lines around her eyes to crinkle and her hand to fly to her mouth to keep her false teeth in place. "Why, just because she said Caleb's wallpaper paste was better than my grits, and that the doilies I starched looked like electrocuted snowflakes? She's been telling me things like that for 50 years. No child, she's a gift from God, the laughter that warms my heart. Besides, you and I both know she's right about the doilies, they do look tortured. Maybe if you spread the cookies out a little, nobody will notice."

# MRS. MURPHY AND THE MOB

❦

A soft tap on the door informed Mrs. Murphy that her ride had arrived. She closed her Bible and laid it on the shaky table beside her chair then went to get her coat. Her only coat was old and inadequate for the weather, so she wore a sweater to keep out the cold. Another person might have worn their best sweater on this occasion, not Mrs. Murphy. She saved her best sweater for church, and she had already worn it earlier in the day to attend her husband's funeral. Her second best sweater was good enough for the company she would be keeping tonight.

She tweaked her cuffs, picked up her handbag, stopped before a mottled mirror to pat her gray hair into place, and opened the apartment door.

The man pacing in the hallway greeted her with forced cheerfulness. "Good even'n there, Miz Murphy!" He was well groomed and expensively dressed. His handmade Italian leather shoes cost more than everything Mrs. Murphy was wearing, but she looked at the man as if he were a cockroach.

"Vinnie," she replied dryly, and turned her back on him to lock the door.

The unappreciated escort nervously stepped aside allowing Mrs. Murphy to go down the stairs ahead of him and bumped into a fire extinguisher hanging on the wall. Startled, he swore and spun around thrusting his hand into his coat. Belatedly realizing what had happened, he laughed self-consciously and pushed his gun back into place. When he looked around, Mrs. Murphy was gone. He heard the dull plopping of her heels on the stairs and tiptoed behind her.

On the third floor landing, a precarious rip in the linoleum flooring lay hidden in the shadow cast by a burned out light bulb, but Mrs. Murphy didn't bother to warn Vinnie. He'd been to building enough times to know it was there.

In the narrow lobby, he flattened himself against the wall and squeezed past her to lean at a clumsy angle, preparing to push open the heavy front door. Just as he started to push, Mrs. Murphy stopped to pull a pair of threadbare gloves over her callused hands. Vinnie faltered and released the bar handle on the door, causing a loud clunk to reverberate in the stairwell. He flinched, and sweat began to roll down his back. When his companion finally looked at the door and squared her shoulders signifying her readiness to go out, he stifled a sigh of relief and shoved on the door straining to hold it as she passed.

Outside, the night sky was black, and bitterly cold air stirred the snowflakes that floated aimlessly in the milky haze around the streetlights. Oblivious to the temperature, Mrs. Murphy calmly walked down the steps and headed for the street, leaving Vinnie to slip and slide as his leather soled shoes skated on the snow-packed concrete.

Half way to the street, he called: "It's icy there, Miz Murphy. Youz'll want to be careful, a woman of your age and all..." The words withered on his tongue, and he awkwardly offered her his arm. She glanced from the sidewalk to his elbow and wordlessly ignored both, confidently treading on with both of her hands firmly clamped on the handbag she carried in front of her.

The street looked deserted, but as she reached the curb, headlights flashed on, and a sleek black town car eased out of its parking place and stopped in front of her. Steadying himself against the car, Vinnie opened the back door, and Mrs. Murphy got in.

The driver craned his neck to see her and chatted with uneasy energy: "Hey, Miz Murphy! That sure was some nice service today, huh? Yeah, that Father George, he done a fine job, a real fine job, huh?"

"Joey," she acknowledged, and turned to stare out the window. Vinnie got in the front seat, and the men exchanged uncomfortable glances.

## The Just and the Unjust Alike

The car moved forward, and the slow blink of streetlights gradually turned into the glare of lights from businesses near the highway. Everything looked surreal through the heavily tinted windows, but Mrs. Murphy's thoughts were far away. The car took a ramp onto the highway and picked up speed as it left the rundown neighborhood behind.

They rode a long time, then slowed, and left the highway for a maze of dark boulevards skirted by uninviting stone walls that shrouded their owner's homes from the eyes of the world. When the car turned into a wide drive and approached a pair of closed gates, Mrs. Murphy thought she saw the red glow of a cigarette being discarded. The car stopped, and a man appeared out of the shadows. Joey put down his window, and the man flicked a flashlight over their faces then stepped back, and the gates swung open.

Several minutes later, the car swung around a circle drive and parked. Graceful stone steps led to a massive house that was tastefully accented by landscape lights. It looked like something out of a magazine. Mrs. Murphy was not impressed.

Vinnie hopped out and opened the door for her. Shunning his help a second time, Mrs. Murphy walked up the wide front steps alone and was admitted to the house by the butler who politely offered to take her coat. She set her handbag down on an antique table, and when she picked it up again, Mrs. Murphy held the handbag in front of her with both hands gripping the top as she followed the butler.

A close inspection of the handbag would have revealed that the strap had broken all the way through leaving only thread holding it together. The butler had seen this, but no mention of Mrs. Murphy's poverty would pass his lips.

He ushered her into a richly furnished room lined with books that no one ever read, and silently left. A slender man, whose once black hair now looked more silver than salt and pepper, stood up to greet her. "Ah, Mary O'Brien," he purred with the familiarity of long acquaintance. "Have a seat, my dear, have a seat. Such a sad occasion, our Patrick will be sorely missed."

Although the two men had known each other all of their lives, Mrs. Murphy had never liked the thought of sharing her late husband with this man, and the steely look in her eyes didn't conceal her sentiments. "Carmine," she responded ignoring the rest of his remarks as she seated herself in the chair opposite his.

His efforts at polite conversation rebuffed, her host got down to business.

"I suppose you know why you're here?" She nodded assent, and as he opened a leather bound ledger on his desk, she pulled a small dogeared notebook from the depths of her handbag. Her notes meant nothing to him, and he smiled patronizingly. "There can be little question as to the amount due."

"Not in my mind," she agreed. "I make the current balance to be $918,742.97 as of 8:33 tonight."

His head jerked up, "I'm afraid you've been misinformed, Mary; although that *is* a nice number."

"No, it's correct," she replied without hesitation. "I've had a long time to learn the way you calculate interest, Carmine, and I've been keeping very careful records. You owe me $918,742.97 and a silver tea service."

Rarely caught off guard, Carmine stared. "I beg your pardon."

"*You* owe *me* $918,742.97, and I want the silver tea service I didn't get for my 25$^{th}$ wedding anniversary.

His eyes narrowed as the hint of a smile eased the harsh lines of his face. Always one to appreciate the ridiculous, Carmine lounged back in his tooled leather chair and began tapping his fingertips together. "You've piqued my curiosity, Mary O'Brien. Perhaps you'll be kind enough to explain how you arrived at this interesting number."

"You should know as well as I do, Carmine, but I'll refresh your memory. Five years ago, you told me that my Patrick owed you a huge amount of money, gambling debts. You said that it was pay up or else. And even if he did pay, you were still going to break his arm, as a warning. Old friend or not, you had to treat him like everybody else who didn't pay on time. You had given your word, and you had to keep it."

He nodded agreement.

"Well, I paid you. I paid you every dollar you said he owed. It took all our savings, selling our house, and everything we had that someone would buy. From my wedding ring to the kitchen clock, I sold it all. It was a nightmare. The amount grew every day, and I felt like I was trying to outrun the devil, but I did it. And I pleaded with you not to break Patrick's arm because how can a tool and die maker work with a broken arm, but you said you had no choice. You had given your word, and you had to keep it, or lose face."

Again he nodded.

"Patrick was heartbroken," she continued with a tinge of sadness. "He couldn't understand how someone who claimed to be his friend would treat him like that? He was worn out and sick, and I begged you...*I begged you*...to just leave us alone. I begged you in the name of Jesus and on the Blessed Virgin Mary, but you wouldn't listen. Then Teresa found out. Your poor wife...she was so upset. We all grew up together, we were friends; she didn't understand how you could do *any* of the things you had done to Patrick. She cried and cried. She cried until she made herself sick and had to go to the hospital. Finally, there at her bedside, as I prayed on my knees for God to comfort her, you gave your word that it was over, you would leave us alone. You swore on the cross that you would not send Vinnie and Joey around to temp Patrick anymore, and Teresa died in peace."

Carmine averted his face, raising one well-manicured hand to shield his eyes.

"That peace lasted for seven months. Patrick got sober, his arm healed, and he went back to work. Every night, he came home at 5:30, and we had supper and read our books. He went to mass with me, and we had a good life...for seven months," she detailed wistfully, but the sentimental mood didn't linger. "Then he sold another invention, and no sooner had the check cleared the bank than here came Vinnie and Joey to take Patrick away from me again. From that day, I've kept every betting slip, every receipt for meals with Vinnie and Joey, every hotel bill for the times he spent with your prostitutes, every scrap of paper I could lay my hands on, and I've tallied the interest. That's how I arrived at the number you find so interesting," and she opened her handbag and took out a thick stack of wrinkled papers and laid them on his desk.

He glanced at the papers, and dismissed them with an insolent wave of his hand. "You're being naïve, Mary O'Brien. Nobody forced Patrick to do anything he didn't want to do," disclaimed Carmine with haughty indifference. "And, surely, you can't hold me accountable for Vinnie and Joey."

"Hah!" she grunted fearlessly showing her contempt for the man behind the desk. "I do hold you accountable, Carmine. It was *you* who gave your word that you would leave us alone, and I do hold you accountable for Vinnie and Joey. Everybody knows they don't breathe unless you say so. My Patrick was a persuadable man, I know that. When he wasn't thinking about gears and calculations, it was like he didn't have thoughts of his own and needed somebody to give him ideas. Well, you gave him ideas, Carmine, bad ideas."

The truth stung, and color rushed into Carmine's face as he leaned forward with his fingers digging into the arms of his chair. "It was business, Mary O'Brien, business. My wife was sick, and I had to provide for her."

"Provide for her! What a miserable excuse to sop your conscience with! Do you think that's the kind of business Teresa wanted you to be in?"

"I kept her in luxury."

"You kept her in hell! You fed her food stolen from the mouths of babies she couldn't have, and you clothed her with the tears of young women you forced into prostitution. Will you never understand that a woman of faith like Teresa would gladly have starved to death, rather than hurt one of those precious lambs?"

"Ssst!" he hissed contemptuously. "You only say that because you hated being poor."

"Oh, Carmine, don't be simple. I didn't mind being poor. I minded being poor when I didn't have to be. I minded living on stale bread while the money my husband earned kept Vinnie and Joey in steaks and custom suits. What I *hated* was being childless and alone while my husband slept with your prostitutes."

"Then you should have married a better man," he threw at her.

"I married a weak man," she acknowledged, "but my poor Teresa, Teresa married a parasite."

His face turned ashen, and he warned in a venomous whisper: "Tread lightly, Mary O'Brien."

Unintimidated, she countered: "Mary O'Brien was an idealistic girl who thought she would be a nurse and make the world a better place. I've been Mrs. Murphy, hospital cleaning lady, for forty years. The closest I ever got to nursing was cleaning up the messes a man like you causes but never touches. Mary O'Brien tried to do everything in her own strength and was afraid of people like you. *Mrs. Murphy* knows that God the Father protects her, and that she can do all things through Jesus Christ who strengthens her; and I *will* have justice!" she declared furiously slamming her fist down on his desk. "I'll have what is fair according to your rules, Carmine. You...*you* gave me your word then you broke it, and I expect you to make things right. It's too late for Patrick, too late to have children, too late to have a twenty-fifth wedding anniversary party; but it's not too late for justice!"

Her fearless determination wearied him. He knew she would not be silenced, and she was not a person he could simply make disappear. Mary

O'Brien might be a girl most of the world had forgotten, but Mrs. Murphy, the cleaning lady who knelt by patient's beds and prayed, was a legend he could not conquer.

Admitting defeat, he held up his hand signaling capitulation, and she put the stack of papers back in her handbag and stood up. "Tomorrow, or I'll have to make adjustments."

He nodded, fumingly aware that he was being served in his own sauce.

"And Carmine," she added lowering her voice meaningfully, "I never want to see Vinnie or Joey again. Not ever."

"As you wish Mary...Murphy," he conceded with a slight bow and summoned the butler. "Take Mrs. Murphy home and send Vinnie and Joey to me. Tell them to come the back way. Oh, and pack up the silver tea service that my wife liked, it belongs to Mrs. Murphy now."

If the butler knew that this unpretentious guest had just bearded the lion in his own den, his face did not show it. He escorted her back to the foyer where he offered her a chair then excused himself while he went to carry out his instructions.

As she waited, Mrs. Murphy's mind grew peaceful, and she realized that she was absentmindedly stroking her handbag and smiled. Like the handbag, her faith had become tired and battered. She knew that most people would have discarded both a long time ago, but she had refused to let go.

## The Just and the Unjust Alike

When it seemed that she was hanging on by a thread, Mary had prayed harder and gripped her faith with both hands, carrying it before her like a shield. "Troubles come and troubles go," she thought, "but the love of the Lord goes on forever."

When the butler returned, he found her quietly singing a song of praise. Once again, he helped her with her coat, then accompanied her down the stone steps to the car. A fresh covering of snow had fallen, and the man offered Mrs. Murphy his arm. Gladly taking it, she thanked him for his thoughtfulness and asked: "Where do I know you from? You look very familiar."

"The hospital," he replied; "my grandmother, Sarah Jamieson, was there for several weeks, you used to pray with her. She never forgot that, and neither have I."

"Oh, I remember Sarah. And what's your name, dear?"

"Michael," he answered returning her smile.

"Well Michael, if it's alright with you, I'd like to sit in the front seat so we can visit on the way back to town."

"I'd like that very much," he agreed warmly.

The miles passed pleasantly, but as the car glided to a stop in front of her building, Mrs. Murphy clasped her friend's forearm. "Michael, dear," she said with an edge of concern in her voice, "do you think it's wise to work for a man like Carmine?"

His eyes twinkled, and he leaned towards her winking enigmatically: "Not to worry, Mrs. Murphy. I'm right where I'm supposed to be."

In her apartment again, a very tired Mrs. Murphy sat down with a cup of tea she had made with her new tea service, and relaxed. What a day, but God is faithful and she rejoiced in His love. When she picked up her Bible, it fell open to Luke 18 (NKJV):

*[1] Then He spoke a parable to them, that men always ought to pray and not lose heart, [2] saying: "There was in a certain city a judge who did not fear God nor regard man. [3] Now there was a widow in that city; and she came to him, saying, 'Get justice for me from my adversary.' [4] And he would not for a while; but afterward he said within himself, 'Though I do not fear God nor regard man, [5] yet because this widow troubles me I will avenge her, lest by her continual coming she weary me.' 6 Then the Lord said, "Hear what the unjust judge said. 7 And shall God not avenge His own elect who cry out day and night to Him, though He bears long with them? 8 I tell you that He will avenge them speedily. Nevertheless, when the Son of Man comes, will He really find faith on the earth?"*

# BUBBA'S GIRL

"What're we going to do about this?"
"I don't think there is anything we can do. This is 1974, not the Middle Ages. Besides, we're only cousins, second cousins at that, and Bubba is not a child. What is he twenty-eight?"

"Weak spirited people never think there's anything to be done in a crisis. Second cousin or not, Bubba is family. We can't sit around like a scurry of squirrels perched on a power line and just watch while he makes a mess of his life," stated Tessie Lou who worked for the Conservation Department. "This is his territory, and you know as soon as he gets out of the Army, he'll come back here to nest."

Surprisingly, none of the other five women sitting around the kitchen table took offense at Tessie Lou's remarks. Having grown up with her, they knew that she was blunt not malicious, and agreed that something needed to be done about Bubba, but what?

"Maybe they won't give him permission to get married. Vietnamese war brides are *very* unpopular, and it's difficult to get a sponsor. She has have to have a sponsor over here, you know," offered Mary Beth hopefully.

"Too late," informed Georgia whose father was pastor of the local Lutheran church. "That left-wing, radical thinking, Bible spouting, hippie loving, commune church over at New Athens has already taken up the girl's cause."

"Oh for God's sake, Georgia, they're Methodists, and they had an *ashram* not a commune!" corrected Olivia. "Papa says Anh, that's her name, Anh, was an interpreter and saved a lot of American lives. He also says she's some sort of Christian, not like us of course, because you know they do things differently on the other side of the world and all. Do you think their Jesus has almond shaped eyes?"

Tessie Lou blinked, and wisely sidestepped that temptation. "We need a plan," she declared, "or this will be just like the time our dear cousin wanted to save that baby raccoon and got the whole town involved, when all he needed was a ladder. Bubba may be dim, but he's persuasive. Nobody can resist him when he pours on the charm."

"I wonder if he would enjoy being governor?" mused Georgia.

"Rabbit trail, Georgie, rabbit trail!" pointed out Tessie Lou.

"He's very handsome," sighed Ruby with a perfected toss of her almost natural blond locks.

"Perhaps I should marry Bubba, our children would be beautiful."

"And dumb!" added Tessie Lou, who oddly enough happened to be Ruby's sister.

Unphased, Ruby shrugged her delicate shoulders, and would have drifted back into her usual narcissistic preoccupation with shopping and seduction, if her sister hadn't continued loudly expounding on the family tree, and how it was already overburdened with cousins who had married. Rejected *and* criticized, Ruby felt unloved, and her bottom lip quivered ominously.

Heading off what threatened to be a lengthy tirade followed by a lengthier burst of retaliatory tears, Mary Beth intervened. "Tessie Lou, those remarks are not becoming on you; and, Ruby, you know you're destined to marry some successful man like a lawyer, or a used car salesman, maybe a politician, so let's just move on, shall we?"

"Like I said," persisted Georgia, "Bubba for Governor."

"Two birds with one stone," agreed Olivia. "State capitol is *all* the way on the other side of the state."

"Stop that, you two," interrupted Mary Beth. "We need a plan that will work quickly. It's time to get Bernadine Strump elected homecoming queen all over again."

"What?"

"Remember in high school when we couldn't stand the thought of Ruby being queen of one more thing? We worked together and got plain little old Bernadine Strump elected homecoming queen. Nothing personal, hon," she interposed patting Ruby's poshly manicured hand, "but nobody should be queen of everything. If the six of us befriend this girl, who would make a stink? If anybody dares to, we'll sic Ruby on them," she added eliciting a trill of laughter from Ruby, and a collective shiver from the others.

So they planned, and the Six Pack, as they were known, welcomed Bubba and Anh with open arms. Bubba went back to work operating heavy equipment, and Anh, whose name means *intellectual brightness*, went to cosmetology school and became a beautician. They built a shop on the back of their house, and it wasn't long before Anh had a long list of clients. And when she didn't like the prices she had to pay for beauty supplies, she started a co-op with other beauty shop owners, and began buying in bulk and selling to the co-op members at reduced prices.

The cousins were her most faithful patrons, partly because it's easier to stay in touch if you all get your hair done on the same day, but mostly, because they genuinely liked Anh, even though some of them didn't always understand her sense of humor. Like one day when rain kept Bubba from working, and Anh asked him to deliver beauty supplies.

"Good husband," she said, "you do this for me today, please? You a good man, God blessed me when you drove bulldozer over my house in Saigon. It was ugly house, not pretty house like this one, and I got to meet you. That make my heart glad! You stop talking to cousins and go now. If you finish early, maybe you go hunting." And she shooed him out the door remarking: "If he think about hunting, maybe he won't play One Hundred Question every place he stop."

"Twenty Questions, Anh, the expression is Twenty Questions," explained Georgia.

"I thought you knew my husband," replied Anh. "He like people and want to know *everything* about them. Talk too much, can't get work done."

Dwelling on herself as usual, Ruby pouted: "Men spend so much time thinking about hunting, don't you mind?"

Unable to resist messing with her, Anh replied: "Oh no, maybe he bring home nice dog for supper. Cat too stringy, dog better." Ruby gasped and the other cousins hid behind their magazines.

"Anh! You don't eat dogs, do you?" pleaded the horrified diva.

"Of course not, you silly girl. No need to eat dogs in this country. But why you crazy Americans eat squirrels when you can get nice fat chicken plucked and ready to cook from the Piggy Wiggy is more than I understand. There more meat on a cat!"

The Tree of Life is a wonderful thing, and Bubba and Anh added two precious branches of their own. Esther Linh became an accomplished plastic surgeon, who charged outrageous fees for elective beauty enhancements, then used the excessive profits to fund humanitarian missions around the world. Her brother, Carmichael Ignatius Montgomery IV, known as Cim to his friends, opened his own accounting firm, managed his sister's finances pro bono, and went hunting with his father. The beauty supply business became so successful, that Bubba retired and spent most of his time congenially keeping other people from getting their work done.

But the Tree of Life never stops changing, and autumn comes to us all.

"Are you sure you want to go out tonight, darlin'? We could stay here and watch a movie or download a Joseph Prince video," suggested Tessie Lou.

"No," replied Anh, "I been sitting in this house for days. Time to get out. We go to nursing home and play Bingo. Brother Cobb call the numbers tonight. It always funny when he forget what he doing and start talking like auctioneer."

"I heard Cobb was in the hospital, is he feeling all better?" inquired Tessie Lou.

"He better. Silly man, he swallow that little plastic thing they put in aspirin bottle to absorb moisture."

"Why on Earth would he do that?"

Mary Beth knew the answer. "He thought it was one of those mini-cameras they use to check your insides."

"Just like a free decoder ring, one in every bottle," mumbled Georgia.

"He's a bachelor," remarked Ruby feigning indifference. "Now that you're single, Anh, I suppose it won't be long till you start trolling for a new husband."

Wisely understanding that we judge other people by ourselves, Anh chose not to take offense at the thoughtless things Ruby said, and instead kindly reassured the ditzy cousin by saying: "You crazy! All that peroxide I put on your hair turn your brain to pickle. I already had best man this town had to offer. You can have rest."

Tessie Lou hugged Anh who pressed her head into the comforting shoulder. She squeezed Tessie Lou and called out to Olivia: "Libby, you get shopping bag full of prizes from porch. Everybody win tonight! We have fun," she promised Tessie Lou hopefully. "And maybe Brother Dave come with his guitar, and we sing songs about Jesus. That make us feel better."

The last one out the door, Anh paused to straighten a picture of Bubba. "You a good man, husband. You talk too much, but first question you ask me after you drove bulldozer over my house in Saigon was: 'If I'd been killed, did I know if I go to Heaven and be with Jesus?' All these years, you never stop asking strangers if they know Jesus. You a good man, and I glad God gave you to me."

# Not Yet

If you've had a stroke and one side of your body doesn't work, propelling a wheelchair down a busy hallway would ordinarily be a challenge. However, ordinary is not a word that applies to Mrs. Nellie Hopper. A stroke may have complicated her life, but it hadn't diminished her desire to help people or impaired her sense of humor. Some folks go to the nursing home to die, Miss Nellie had settled in determined to live whatever life she has left to the fullest.

Today, she was on a mission, and as she slowly worked her way down the hall, she stopped frequently to pat hands and give encouraging smiles. You see, Miss Nellie understood that the journey is as important as the destination. At the main nurse's station, she parked herself out of the way and patiently waited. Well aware of her presence, the head nurse continued to check charts, but began to discuss Miss Nellie with the other nurse.

"She's back."

"Oh no, not *her*!"

"Mmhuh, sitting over there like a sweet little angel."

"Maybe if we ignore her, she'll go away."

"Huh! Don't kid yourself, she didn't pull herself all the way down here for no reason. Nope, she's up to something."

"What do you think she wants? Do we have any chocolate?"

"Spare yourself the trouble, girl. She doesn't want your chocolate, she wants a new roommate. Don't you, sweet lady?"

The twinkle in Miss Nellie's eyes and the lopsided smile that deepened the creases on the active side of her face were difficult to resist, and the nurses smiled back. A new roommate was exactly what she wanted.

"What happened to her last roommate?" asked Nurse Carrie.

"Mrs. Truvey? Poor woman, she didn't stand a chance. Miss Nellie encouraged her so much, she got well and went home. Isn't that right?"

Miss Nellie dropped her head a little, and one soaring eyebrow deprecatingly acknowledged the truth, and expressed: "Well, yes, that's exactly what I did."

"If she keeps that up, we'll be out of business," teased Nurse Carrie.

"Oh no," assured her older colleague, "we'll have to stay on just to funnel people to her." They all

*Not Yet*

laughed, and Nurse Janet stepped out from behind the desk to give Miss Nellie a hug and whisper in her ear: "Next good candidate that comes in, dear. Let's pray. Thank you, Father, for bringing Miss Nellie to us, and for sending another person who needs her special kind of help. In Jesus' name, amen."

Miss Nellie hugged her back then held out her clutched hand. Nurse Janet extended her palm, and two Hershey's Kisses dropped into it.

As their interesting friend rolled away, Janet slipped one of the Kisses to Carrie and earnestly remarked: "I love that woman. She does more to rehabilitate the patients here than all the medicine in the world."

Three days later, a transfer ambulance delivered Miss Nellie's new roommate. Before her illness, Peggy had been an active middle-aged woman with a full life and a strong spirit. She had gone to the hospital for gallbladder surgery, and contracted a Super Bug virus that had stripped her of everything but the most basic drive to keep living. Exhaustion and lethargy ruled her days and dulled her mind. When she could think, she honestly wondered if death might not be her best option, but it was not her decision to make. God was not ready for her to depart this life, so she continued to drift along in a foggy limbo.

The short trip from the hospital to the nursing home fatigued Peggy, and she slept most of the first day. That evening, her husband and sons came to visit. The murmur of male voices mingled with the scent of fresh aftershave awakened Peggy, and she opened her eyes.

"Hi, Mom, good to see you," greeted her oldest son in a hushed voice. Nathan gave his mom a slight hug and gently kissed her cheek, as though he thought she would break.

"Hi, gorgeous, I have a message for you," teased her other son, Sam. He blew a raspberry kiss on her cheek, saying it was from her favorite grandson. He only had one son, so she didn't have to guess who he meant, and she smiled weakly.

Last to her side was her husband of forty plus years. Harvey gave her an awkward pat on the shoulder and a peck on the cheek. He took her return greeting for granted, and the three men sat down. They made a few cursory remarks about Peggy's new room, then the discussion turned to farming. Since they all worked together on the farms they owned, it was a natural progression. Nathan took care of the livestock, Sam handled the grain and row crops, Harvey and, until her illness, Peggy, oversaw the business in general and made all the major decisions.

Harvey never got tired of farming, but Peggy was ready to step down and let the next generation take over. She reasoned that they had two competent, grown sons who would do a good job. Sure, they would make a few mistakes, that's to be expected. They'd learn and do better going forward. Harvey disagreed and stubbornly resisted any change. As a result, every conversation ended in an argument, and tonight was no exception.

The discussion had started out benignly enough, then differing ideas led to a clash of wills, and Peggy seethed. It was the same-old-same-old she had been subjected to for years, only worse. Now, she was a captive to her bed and couldn't leave the room when she'd had enough. Too weak to tell the men to knock it off, she did the only thing she had the strength for, and poked her hand at the ugly pink plastic water glass on the hospital table over her bed.

The glass hit the floor and bounced with a hollow clatter. Nathan jumped to retrieve it. "I'm sorry, Momma, do you want a drink?"

No, she did not want a stupid drink. She wanted them to take their stupid argument out of earshot, and let her die in stupid peace. Unable to speak her mind, she took a few sips of the water Nathan was offering, and breathed a sigh of relief when Harvey announced that Mom was tired, so they'd better head out.

Her son's kissed her goodbye, and Harvey brushed his lips over hers, then remembered that she hated half-hearted kisses and doubled back to give his wife a real kiss, effectively making amends without knowing it.

The next day, Peggy felt rested and started to take notice of her surroundings. The room was nondescript, but it faced south and pleasant sunshine filled it most of the day. Nurse Janet came by to check on

*The Just and the Unjust Alike*

the new arrival, and to introduce her to Miss Nellie. At least her roommate wouldn't be argumentative thought Peggy.

Things got more interesting around evening when Miss Nellie's daughter arrived with contraband. The dietitian at the nursing home ruled the entire facility with an iron ladle. Although a genuinely nice person, the stern authoritarian firmly believed that unhealthy food brought in by misguided visitors derailed the recovery process. Therefore, she adamantly insisted that no outside food be allowed. Miss Nellie silently rebelled. It wasn't that the dining room food was bad, for "institution food" it was exceptionally good. Miss Nellie simply liked her daughter's cooking better, especially her soup, and today, Andrea had smuggled in a thermos of chicken vegetable.

One of the aides had already been around to feed Peggy a protein shake and a few bites of mashed something, and she was lying with her eyes closed pretending to be asleep. She thought she was doing a good job of playing opossum until something Andrea said made her laugh. Andrea would talk to her mother then interpret the silent woman's response from her facial expressions and hand gestures. Whether through genuine misunderstanding or a deliberate attempt at humor, she would say ridiculous things, and you couldn't help laughing. Knowing she was caught, Peggy opened her eyes and smiled.

## Not Yet

Andrea stepped over to introduce herself and offer a taste of the contraband soup. "There's some chicken soup left. Would you like to try a little?"

Since it was easier to eat the soup than attempt to politely refuse, Peggy accepted the spoon and got a surprise. The soup was very good. It was flavorful without being salty, and she enjoyed it very much, willingly opening her mouth for more and gratefully swallowing all that Andrea offered her.

Full and content, Peggy drifted off to sleep, hoping she had adequately thanked her new friend for the treat.

Peggy woke up to early morning light and a jumble of words that might be a song. When her eyes focused, she saw Miss Nellie sitting by the window with a book open on her lap. Her good arm was raised, and she was singing with a depth of feeling that told Peggy her roommate was praising God. The words didn't make any sense, but whether her indecipherable language was the product of the clot in her brain or whether she was praying in the Spirit, Peggy knew that God understood perfectly, and silently joined in raising her shaky hands as far off the covers as she could. It felt good to be worshipping in fellowship again, and Peggy's spirits lifted.

Later in the day, Peggy's mood suffered a set back when the physical therapist came to help her exercise. Kevin's inexhaustible flow of cheeriness grated on her nerves, and she would have lashed

## The Just and the Unjust Alike

out at him, except for the comedian who shared her room. Well aware of the struggle Peggy faced, Miss Nellie encouraged her by making crazy faces and outlandish gestures, behind Kevin's back. He wasn't fooled and would good-naturedly remark: "I saw that!"

Laughter does make you feel better, and Peggy grudgingly admitted to herself that both aspects of the workout had given her more energy.

The days passed, but while Peggy was growing stronger on the inside, she didn't appear to be making much progress on the outside. Harvey felt discouraged. He worried that his wife was not going to recover. His breaking point came one afternoon when he arrived shortly after the beautician had left. The lady had cut and washed Peggy's hair then put a little blush on her cheeks and given her a touch of lipstick. Peggy felt more like her old self, but when Harvey saw her, the thought that she had died and was laid out for her funeral grabbed his mind. He burst into tears.

"No! No!" he moaned.

Peggy opened her eyes and knew in a heartbeat what he was thinking. Ashamed of himself for crying but unable to stop, he stood by her bed and sobbingly asked: "Are you going to leave me?"

"Not yet," she whispered doing her best to hold out her arms.

The strength he'd been walking in dissolved, and Harvey collapsed onto her shoulder. She was the love of his life, and he missed her terribly. He tried to be strong, but the fear that Peggy was slipping away weighed heavily on him. Thinking that this could be the last time he held her in his arms, Harvey slid onto the bed and pulled Peggy close as he wept.

Three times, she had only seen this man cry three times. Every speck of determination in Peggy galvanized. She had to get better for Harvey, he needed her; and even though he could annoy the socks off of her, she loved him and wanted to be with him.

Pushing herself to act, Peggy tightened her arms. Harvey felt her move and pulled her hand to his lips. "You're my best girl. I don't know what I'd do without you," he confessed.

"Only girl," she clarified. He gave a choke of laughter and kissed her hand again.

They fell asleep and slept the best they had since this whole ordeal had begun. They woke up at supper time, and Harvey stayed to eat with Peggy, feeding her small bites of food from his plate and talking with her about grandkids and neighborhood news. Miss Nellie tactfully found other places to be, and rejoiced in the knowledge that *both* of her new friends were making great progress.

After supper, Harvey turned on the television, and they watched a program Peggy liked. She fell asleep before the end of the show, and Harvey carefully tucked her up for the night making sure to leave the blankets loose near her feet, just in case she wanted to stick her toes out. He wasn't sure she had the strength, but he wanted her to have the option.

As Harvey walked down the hall to leave, an elderly man suffering from dementia held out a scrap of paper. "This one is for you. Thus saith the Lord, *this one* is for you!"

Harvey had a kind heart, and he took the paper warmly thanking the old man as they shook hands. "Poor old soul," he thought making sure the outside door latched, so the alarm would go off if the old gent tried to leave the building. He started to put the paper in his pocket then paused under a vapor light to read it. At first, the shaky scrawl eluded him. Oh, it was upside down; he turned it and read: "Rev 2:3-4"

He knew it was from the Bible, after all, Harvey was a deacon. But off the top of his head, he couldn't remember the exact quote. His mind tried to jump to farming and his plans for the next day, but the verses teased him. Unable to push them aside, he popped the trunk of his car and reached for the Bible he kept there. As the trunk lid lifted, the light came on, and Harvey chuckled. The trunk of this car was nicer than the seats of the cars he used to drive. He had worked a long time to afford a car like this, and he was proud of himself and Peggy for the good stewardship practices that allowed them to have nice things. At least he was, until he unzipped the expensive leather Bible case and looked up the verses. Harvey was immediately convicted, and his heart sank.

Revelation 2:3-4 "...*you have persevered and have patience, and have labored for my name's sake and have not become weary. Nevertheless I have this against you, that you have left your first love.*"

Harvey had grown away from God. Fifty years ago, the inexpensive Bible that he cherished rode in the front seat with him. He would never have put it in the trunk, much less have left it there for weeks at a time. Harvey had become arrogant, no longer feeling the need to study God's Word. He knew the Word. Well, he knew a boat load of scriptures that he threw out with great confidence. He would have been deeply offended if anyone had questioned his faith, but in truth, now he worshipped more at the altar of *Harvey Worked Hard* than he did at the feet of the Lord.

He shut the trunk taking the Bible with him, and as he got in the car, he thought about how it had become *the* Bible to him not *his* Bible, and his spirit grieved. It was not difficult to trace the path that had taken him off course, life happens Only now, he knew that God was calling him back, and Harvey wanted to return to the place where he had first met God.

He didn't see as well as he used to, but the early spring night didn't intimidate the tired man. He knew the roads by heart, and turn after turn brought him closer to his roots. He passed the old home place where house he grew up in had stood, and in less than a mile, arrived at an old church. The congregation had dispersed decades ago, and nobody used the one room building any more. It should probably be torn down, but nobody had the heart to make that decision.

Harvey was one of the few people left who remembered when the little church had thrived. And as he turned off the road and parked near what remained of the hitching posts, his mind went back. Stepping out of his car, his memory began to replay the sights and sounds from that night, the night that changed his life.

People had come from miles around for a tent revival. Curious, Harvey had finished his chores and strolled over to see why so many people would go out of their way to hear a preacher on a week night. Gangly and quiet, he had respectfully nodded to folks as he paced himself with the crowd that was narrowing to pass through the gate into the field beside the church. Earlier in the day, a big canvas tent had been set up in the mowed hay field; and in the dusk, it glowed with light from the bare bulbs that swayed back and forth on black electrical wires strung between the tent poles.

Rows of straw bales provided seating, and some of the more well to do people had brought their own wooden folding chairs. Sitting down on a bale and looking around to see if any of his friends were there, young Harvey had thought that one day, he'd like to own one of those fancy wooden folding chairs, so he wouldn't have to sit on the prickly straw. Now, he owned the field and all the land around it, but in many ways, he still felt poor.

The meeting had begun with hymns banged out on an old upright piano, and Harvey sang along belting out the lyrics when he knew them, and soundlessly moving his lips when he didn't. Then the pastor from the little church had prayed and introduced the guest speaker. The visiting evangelist was barely out of his twenties, and Harvey liked the way he talked. He didn't yell or pound his fist on the pulpit the way Brother Marvin did, the young man spoke to the audience the way you talk to a friend, and the sincere tone of his voice drew Harvey in and planted a God seed in the boy's heart that took root and grew.

At the end of the service, the young pastor invited every one who wanted to be saved to come forward. Harvey knew the invitation was for him, so he had stirred up his courage and walked to the front where he knelt down on both knees and gave his life to Christ. Now standing in that same field, Harvey looked up at the night sky lit by stars that only God could count, and he apologized to the Maker of the Universe for having forgotten his roots.

Harvey had had knee surgery, and it was difficult for him to get up and down. As a deacon, he frequently prayed at the altar, and had convinced himself that he knelt on one knee to make sure he could get up without disrupting the service. But the truth he knew in his heart was that he knelt on one knee because he was only half-surrendered to God. Half of his heart had become too proud to bend. Tonight, he was getting down on both knees, even if he had to crawl on his elbows to a fence post in order to stand up again.

The dry grass cushioned his landing, and he dusted his hands, nervously wondering what to say. It had been such a long time since Harvey had talked to God in an intimate way, that he wasn't sure how to start. Then the Holy Spirit reminded him of a scripture, and the words began to flow: "Please, Father, *restore to me the joy of Your salvation*, Psalm 51:12. Remind me, Lord, remind me how I felt when You were the most important thing in the world to me. I miss Your presence!" and for the second time that day, Harvey wept out of fear that he had been at risk of losing someone very important to him.

It was after 10:00 when he got back into his car. It didn't matter though, Harvey picked up his cell phone and made three calls. The first was to Nathan who answered sharply: "Daddy, is everything okay?" Instead of snapping at his soft-hearted son for being a worrier, Harvey reassured him, explaining that Mom was doing better and that they had eaten supper together and watched TV.

"I called because I want to meet with you and Sam in the morning, 8:00 at the office. Good night, Nate, and, son, I'm proud of you."

His call to Sam went much faster, although he was not to know that the second he hung up, Sam called his brother, and they talked for an hour trying to figure out what was going on with Dad.

The third call was to the young man who rented the house that Harvey and Peggy had built on their favorite farm. Peggy preferred that modern brick ranch house to the rambling Victorian mansion they currently occupied. Harvey rationalized that since the big house was located on land at the center of their farming operation, it made sense for the people who ran the operation to live there. Peggy knew that was a lot of hot air, but she loved Harvey in spite of his pride, and they wrestled with the stairs and the challenges generated by living in more house than you need.

Davis had grown up with Harvey's boys, attending the same church and schools. As kids, they spent so much time together that he was more like a cousin than a neighbor. He was a good man with degree in agribusiness and had worked for a large accounting firm until the downturn in the economy eliminated his job. He helped some of the local farmers with their taxes and worked with Nathan and Sam from time to time, but he needed a fulltime job to support his wife and their two children, as well as the two foster children his family hoped to adopt.

Happy at the prospect of a day's work, Davis gladly agreed to meet Harvey in the morning, and told his wife he had the feeling that some of their prayers were about to be answered. Gratefully expectant, the young couple knelt beside their bed and thanked God for his faithfulness.

Morning meetings were common, but the three younger men were struck dumb by Harvey's opening statement.

"As of today, I'm retiring. I want to spend more time with Mom, and you know she's been telling me to let you take over for a long time. My last act as president is to hire Davis as chief financial officer and general manager. Neither of you likes that sort of work, and it's important. The salary may not be what you're used to, Davis, but you and Jenny will live here in the big house, and your utilities and vehicle expenses will all be paid. Peggy and I'll move back to the ranch house. She likes it better, and frankly, I've had enough of those blasted stairs! You guys can work out the business details among yourselves. Sam, I think you should be president, unless you want to take over, Nathan. You're the oldest."

"Oh, hell no!" exclaimed the quiet older brother who understood animals better than people. "Ssssam can do it," he stuttered adamantly.

They all laughed, but Harvey gently reprimanded him saying: "Mind your words now. Without Mom here, we've gotten slack," and he pointed at the Swear Jar which Sam reached for and dusted off with the sleeve of his Carhartt jacket while his brother got out his wallet. You were supposed to drop in a quarter for each swear word; Nathan folded a $20 bill and slipped it through the slot. When the onlookers stared at him, Nathan held up three blackened finger nails that had been smashed by the lid of hog feeder.

They briefly discussed how responsibilities would be divided, then Harvey stunned his sons a second time by actually leaving. He was going to help Peggy do physical therapy. Half-an-hour later, when her husband walked into Peggy's room and rolled up his sleeves, the pucker between her eyebrows conveyed the question in her mind.

"What am I doing here? I'm gonna help you do physical therapy. Nurse Janet introduced me to Kevin, and I thought it would be a good thing for me to run interference before you get strong enough to kick him through a window."

Peggy smiled, acknowledging his accurate reading of her character and asked: "Who's running the farm?"

"We have two competent grown sons who'll do just fine," he replied quoting her words back to her. "By the way, I retired this morning, you should too, then we can start taking those trips you've been planning. Oh, Davis is going to be CFO and general manager, so he and Jenny will have to trade houses with us."

Tears filled Peggy's eyes. In the past, any time she had suggested that they retire, Harvey would say: "Let's work a few more years then retire and build our dream house." Disappointed, Peggy would counter that she had already built her dream house, and that somebody else was living in it. Now that she was moving back to the house she loved, she was even more motivated to get better. Kevin popped into the room before she could comment, and the rest of the morning was filled with stretches and pushes.

Following Kevin's instructions, Harvey was massaging his way up Peggy's thigh. When he glanced at her face, she shot him a flirtatious look that made him turn bright red and retreat to work the muscles in her foot. She laughed at her husband's spurt of modesty and mouthed: "Sixty-four Chevy."

The private joke made him laugh and turn even redder. After furtively glancing to see if anyone was looking, Harvey raised her foot to his mouth and playfully bit a toe. Peggy laughed out loud and tried to pull her foot away; Harvey held on tight and pressed the foot to his heart. She was back. The girl he loved was back, and he was holding on.

It was not easy, and there were some setbacks, but Peggy did her exercises and ate Andrea's soup, doing all that she could to get better. She was blessed with two wonderful daughter-in-laws who loved her and got along well. And while Peggy recuperated, they painted the rooms in the ranch house, and got Nathan and Sam to move their parent's furniture, and rearrange it several more times than the men thought absolutely necessary. The house was ready when Peggy was, and all she had to do now was go home and enjoy herself.

Telling Miss Nellie goodbye was difficult. "I can't thank you enough," said Peggy. "I could never have done this without you, and I thank God for blessing me with your friendship." Miss Nellie blew her a kiss and waved as another roommate moved on.

While the orderlies cleaned Peggy's side of the room, Miss Nellie pulled herself along the busy hallway to the nurses station. Having just released Peggy, Nurse Janet fully expected to see Miss Nellie and announced to Nurse Carrie: "She's back."

"Again! What do you think she wants?"

In reply, Miss Nellie held up the going away present Peggy's daughter-in-laws had made for her, it was a hot pink bedazzled Vacancy sign.

# SOMEBODY'S DADDY

What a lovely night to follow a wonderful day. The Bride pulled a rose from one of the table arrangements, and inhaled deeply, as she added its sweetness to her memories. Weddings are so full that time can easily become a pleasant blur, and she didn't want that to happen. Every little detail added to the magic, and she gathered as many as she could.

They were married. Wow, they were married! That would take some getting use to. Dinner was over, music was playing, the guests were enjoying themselves, and all she had to do was relax. She looked for Hubby and saw him straddling a chair with his arms resting on the back, as he talked with a group of his college buddies. Their eyes met, and he smiled. It *was* a lovely night.

The only thing that would have made it better, would have been for her mom and step-dad to be there. Both had passed away, one right after the other, about a year ago, and even though she knew they were in Heaven, she missed them. Her friends

*Somebody's Daddy*

were so good, and her new in-laws were so terrific, that until now, she had gotten through the day without one regret, but tonight, she wished for some family of her own to share her joy.

As she savored the moment, a familiar-looking man approached her and held out a card. You expect that at wedding receptions, but she couldn't place him. He was middle-aged, tall, and handsome; he was not the kind of person you forget, and that bugged her. Something about his eyes intrigued her, and she studied him as she held out her hand to shake his.

"I'm so proud of you," he said earnestly.

That meant a lot to her, and she didn't know why. "Thank you," she replied warmly. "I'm sorry, I know I should know you, but I don't recall your name," she confessed.

"I'd be very surprised if you did," he answered humbly. "I wish you all the best though, and I hope you don't mind me saying this, but you look like your mother. Only, I think, prettier."

The Bride laughed. "Were you a friend of Mom's?"

"I knew her before you were born, and come to think of it, I hooked her up with your step-father. They were good people."

He handed her the card he was holding and started to walk away, seemingly reluctant to intrude on her moment. She had to know who he was, and quickly opened the envelop. The card was thick and

## The Just and the Unjust Alike

elegant, the kind you give someone you care a great deal about. It wasn't signed, there was just a little note wishing her well, and an exceptionally generous cashier's check. Her eyes widened, but she pushed aside the check and stared at the handwriting. She'd seen that writing before. Her first semester at college, she'd been goofing off, and a note came that said: "You've had your fun, now it's time to study." She had gotten the point and made the dean's list every semester. She saw that writing again when her step-dad died. Among the cards was an unsigned note encouraging her to be brave for her mom. And when her mom had unexpectedly passed, a note came reassuring the heartbroken young woman that she was not alone.

Suddenly, she knew who he was and called out: "Wait, please!" Afraid to voice the thoughts jostling her mind, she retrieved a small satin bag from the pocket hidden in the skirt of her gown, and showed him a strip of faded blue hanky. In reply, he reached for his wallet and pulled out the yellowed corner torn from a child's school paper.

She touched it, and his hand closed over hers as they remembered the first time they met. He had paused in front of a liquor store to finish his cigarette. He'd been working a job in a dark windowless building and just wanted to be outside for awhile. The sky was overcast, and the smog was thick, but he didn't care, he didn't care about much of anything. He turned to go into the store and caught his reflection in the window. Romance novels would have described him as *ruggedly handsome with raven black hair, and dark, enigmatic eyes that cut to a woman's soul.* Bullshit, he saw the real man, a satyr: a cold, heartless, seducer.

A wobbly speck of color in the glass drew his attention, and he looked across the street. A little girl about five was plodding along singing snatches of a children's song, and waving her school paper to keep time. A lock of mousey brown hair was slipping out of a cheap plastic barrette, her coat was too small, and her shoes were too big. One dingy anklet had worked its way down into her shoe, and he saw her bare heel with every floppy step. The hem of her dress hit above her knees, and those little legs had to be cold. A kinder man would have pitied the poor little wretch. He was not a kinder man.

He knew who she was, he just didn't care.

As he watched, the toe of one clumsy shoe snagged on a crack in the sidewalk pitching her forward into a full-length splat on the concrete. The impact knocked the air out of her, and he waited to see what would happen as the child rolled over and sat up, struggling to catch her breath.

Tears, yeah, there were tears, not that he cared, life's full of pain. And if that had been all there was to it, he'd have gone his way without giving her a second thought. But there was something deeper in her sorrow. She cried tears of abandonment; tears for no one, because no one would be coming to comfort her. She cried tears of resignation because this was her lot in life, and she had no expectation that it would change. She sat in the dirt rocking back and forth trying to comfort herself, and cried tears of hopelessness. No one should be hopeless at five-years-old, and it irritated him that this child in particular should feel that way.

"Ah crap," he swore flicking the butt of his cigarette aside and crossing the street.

She couldn't see through her tears, and when he knelt beside her, the child cowered and tried to scoot away. Her reaction annoyed him.

"I'm not gonna hurt you!" he growled. She flinched, and he realized that there wasn't anything reassuring in his tone and hesitated.

She blinked away the tears and shudderingly asked: "Are you somebody's daddy?"

"Looks that way," he frowned. "Are you hurt?" She held out the palm that had hit the sidewalk the hardest. The skin was torn in several places, and grit stuck to the blood. He fished in his hip pocket for a hanky and gently brushed off the dirt. She drew in a sharp hissing breath but didn't pull away. He turned her hand over to check the back and thought how small it looked in his. The dimples on her knuckles brought home to him that she was still a baby. "What else?" he asked, striving for indifference.

Her other hand, the one that had carried the school paper, had scraped knuckles and was cupped over her right knee. She stiffened and moved that hand. The outer layer of skin had been ground off of her kneecap and bright red blood oozed out. She grimaced.

"That's pretty gross," he acknowledged, "but it'll be okay."

She looked in his eyes, then echoed: "Okay," innocently taking him at his word.

He shook out the hanky, tore a strip off one end, and folded the rest to make a pad. He asked if she was ready, then laid the pad over the wounded kneecap and tied the strip of cloth around her leg. "Where do you live?"

She pointed, and he knew the child must be living with her mother's aunt. When he held out his hands, she expected him to stand her up, so she could hobble the rest of the way by herself. Instead, he guided her arms around his neck and held her against his chest, as he crooked an arm under her hips being careful not to bump the hurt knee.

They took off, his long strides covering the distance much faster than her little legs could have trudged. With every step, he grew angrier. The aunt lived too far from the girl's school, and this neighborhood sucked. The child's mother should be taking better care of her. How much of a burden could one little kid be?

As part of his job, the man moved large pieces of equipment and worked with heavy wrenches; the girl weighed less than his tool box, but after he had carried her a few blocks, his arm ached. He stopped

## The Just and the Unjust Alike

at a drug store to buy a pack of cigarettes, and it hit him that he probably spent more money on smokes and booze each week than the little girl's mother could afford to spend on food for a month. Instead of cigarettes, he asked the lady behind the counter for a bottle of antiseptic spray, the kind that doesn't sting, and a box of bandages big enough to cover the hurt knee.

Outside, they passed an unpleasant man who leered at the little girl in a way that made her rescuer's skin crawl. Shaken and angry, he instinctively covered the child's back with his hand. Taking care of children was more complicated than her knight had first thought, and it was dawning on him that no matter how strong you are, you can't do it alone.

It started to sprinkle, and when the little girl shivered, he shifted her to the other arm and wrapped his coat over her. She snuggled against his heart, and he quietly swore again.

At the aunt's house, he stood her on the porch and handed her the bag from the drug store telling her that she could make it from there. He started to leave, and a rustling sound reminded him of the school paper he had shoved in his pocket. He handed it to her, and she sighed: "It ripped."

The corner she had been holding when she fell was torn. "Tell you what," he offered, "you keep the big piece, and I'll keep the little piece. How about that?"

She beamed at him. "That way, maybe you won't forget me," she suggested shyly.

"I won't forget you," he promised and walked away. The next day, a flamboyantly dressed woman, who looked suspiciously like a hooker, knocked on the aunt's door, and handed her a bag of clothes mechanically saying that her kid had outgrown these things, and maybe, the little girl who lived here could use them. A few weeks later, the owner of an apartment building close to the grade school stopped at the café where the little girl's mother worked, and offered her an apartment at a huge discount, if she would be willing to clean the hallways in the building. Favor had continued to flow, and it seemed like their Good Angel was finally watching over the little girl and her mother.

"That day changed my life," she whispered.

"It saved mine," he replied.

"Are you somebody's daddy?" she asked breathlessly.

"Yours," he confirmed.

They sat down at a table and held hands while they talked. "Did you send the clothes and help with the apartment by the school?"

"Yes," he chuckled, "I didn't think that hooker would ever remember her lines. And I traded repair work on the some of the landlord's other buildings to make the rent affordable for your mom. I didn't want it to seem too easy, so I had him throw in that part about cleaning the halls."

"Why didn't tell her? I don't understand why you didn't want us to know you were helping."

He looked chagrined. "For one thing, I treated your mom so badly I thought she'd refuse my help. And...well...God had just started working on me, and I was still a selfish jerk. I thought that if your mom knew I was willing to do something, she might asked for more than I wanted to give. I wanted to be able to stop on my terms."

"But you didn't stop, things we needed seemed to always show up at the right time, and I had a full scholarship to college. I'm smart, but not that smart."

"Figured that out did you? Employees' dependents get free tuition, so I got a job at the University. I'm proud of you. You were a good student."

She giggled. "After you sent me that note, you mean!"

"I was watching," he agreed.

"And what about my step-dad? You said you hooked him and Mom up."

"Yeah, I met him at a bar one night. He was sitting there doing a crossword puzzle, and I'd never seen anybody look so out of place. When I said so, he told me that he was a widower and had just moved here for a job. He didn't like bars, but he didn't have any friends. I told him about a pretty waitress who liked crosswords, and the rest was God."

She had to clear her throat. "That was kind of you. They were very happy."

"I owed her that," he said honestly. "And I owe you something too. I didn't think it was right to stick my nose in after you'd made all of your wedding plans, but if it's not too late, I'm really hoping you'll dance with me."

# CALLIOPE JANE

"Would you like a book today, dear?" What do you do when you retire and enjoy good health? You give back. Beth Martin liked to give back by volunteering at a transitional care facility. Most of the people she met loved her visits, and Beth knew that the angry folks were just hurting and did her best to add them to her circle of friends. Today, she noticed a new resident and stopped to get acquainted.

"Hello, may I come in? I'm Beth, the book lady, welcome the fun wing!" She said that to everyone because it's comforting to think you're somewhere special. "How about something to read, we've got magazines and books, and there's a large selection of books on cds if you would rather listen. You could play to them on your lap top," she added noticing a computer on the table beside the bed.

"You're very thoughtful, but I'm not in the mood right now. Perhaps some other time." Although the woman's voice was faint, it was distinctive, and Beth responded excitedly.

"I know you! I mean I know who you are: you're Penelope Werner, the voice of *Calliope Jane*. I loved that program! My friends and I used to listen to it every week. You were our hero," Beth ended reverently.

"Oh heavens, that was decades ago, and I wasn't a hero just a supporting character in a goofy, small town, radio station, soap opera. Most of the time, I sold advertising or worked in the sound booth."

"You were terrific!" insisted Beth unwilling to allow this paragon from her childhood to be diminished. "And when you left, you went to Hollywood."

"Oh yes, I was going to be a star," agreed Ms. Werner sarcastically. "I did a few commercials and some bit parts, not many though. They told me I was too big and too homely to be a leading lady, and that there was already an over abundance of experienced actresses competing for *best friend* roles. No room at the inn, kiddo, so I became a producer. There's nothing heroic about settling for Plan B." The tart edge in her voice smacked of bitterness.

Beth hated that. "I'm not sure how well you see, Ms. Werner," she said, "but I'm no Twiggy, never was. I was loud and awkward, and I got picked on a lot. You gave me ideas outside of my reality and encouragement no one else offered. If Calliope Jane could own a livery stable and a feed store, and be on the town board, there was hope for me. Your real life career was even better, you produced a long string of successful television shows. That's not chopped liver."

"Maybe not," murmured Ms. Werner turning away. "Thank you for stopping by."

Summarily dismissed, Beth left determined to find a way of showing Ms. Werner the positive impact she'd made on her young audience.

Unglamorous but well educated, Penelope Werner had initially declined the role of Calliope Jane, a loud-mouthed buffoon intended as foil for an overly delicate leading lady. The original script made Jane the butt of every joke; Werner didn't want anything to do with the program. The radio station owner had persisted. Werner had the voice he wanted for the part; to get it, he allowed her to rewrite the script turning the boisterous Calliope Jane into a successful business woman with a big heart and a steady stream of wise, albeit corny, sayings:

"You're a blessing or barnacle, it's your choice."

"It's better to be eaten by tigers than trampled by mice."

"Two things float to the top, but only one of them is cream."

And everyone's favorite: "Pretty or plain, use your brain."

Penelope Werner was a beacon on the hill for the 1960's girls stuck in Beth's hometown. She told her listeners that they had the right to choose who they would become, that there is no shame in trying and failing, that making it to the top is about more than getting there, and not to allow themselves to be pigeon holed by looks.

Beth kicked herself. Why hadn't she thought of telling Ms. Werner how much she appreciated Calliope Jane's earthy wisdom before now? It seemed very wrong to have so extensively used the tools and never to have thanked the giver. Well, that was about to change.

On the way home, Beth's mind began to whirl. Ms. Werner's illness wasn't very serious, where would she go after that? In fast succession, Beth went from wondering to planning, and in a matter of minutes had arranged the remainder of Ms. Werner's life. Miss Fix It would see to it that her mentor had a nice place to live surrounded by kind, pleasant people. She wouldn't want for anything, and they would be friends, and...and... STOP!

The big red and white sign said: "STOP!" Beth slammed on her brakes. "Whew!" she breathed. "I wasn't paying attention."

"You're still not," whispered the quiet voice that Beth recognized as God. "What makes you think she needs your money?" He asked gently.

"Nothing," sighed Beth miserably. But that was what Beth did. When she wasn't sure what to do, she threw money at the problem until it went away. Maybe it was time for some fresh thinking.

She drove safely through the intersection and pulled into a parking lot. Okay, rethink this. What had she done? She had seen a need, and with that one little twig, she had begun building without asking the bird if it wanted or even needed a nest. She took a deep breath and tried not to feel the way Peter must have in Mark 9:2-6 when Jesus was transfigured on the mountain. Wanting to help, but nervous and not knowing what to do, Peter had offered to build three tabernacles, one for Jesus, one for Moses and one for Elijah.

"Duh," thought Beth. "If they came all the way from Heaven to see Jesus, wouldn't they want to be in the same tabernacle?"

"Did Jesus *ask* for a tabernacle?"

"No," admitted Beth In the business world, her aggressive personality along with a sharp eye for discerning need and a mind filled with creative solutions had been a blessing. Finding her way in retirement required different skills, but she knew how to simplify things and spent several minutes thanking God for His timely intervention and asking for His guidance.

Feeling that she had a more appropriate handle on the situation, Beth solicited advice from her daughter, then went home and put social networking to work. Within hours, her childhood friends began responding, and the following week, she smiled all the way to the transitional care home.

"Ms. Werner, may I come in?" she asked glowing with excitement. "I have something to show you." Without waiting for a response, she set up her mentor's lap top and turned it on. While it booted up, she helped the elderly woman sit up and find her glasses.

"I suppose you're going to show me this, whatever it is, whether I consent or not," grumbled Ms. Werner.

"That's the plan," chuckled Beth. "You taught us *not* to take no for an answer."

"How shortsighted of me."

"Oh no, it's served me well. Before I retired, I owned the largest commercial real estate company in the tri-state metro-plex. Thanks to your inspiration, I was very successful, and you have quite a few more spiritual god-daughters who would like to share with you."

The computer screen came alive with a You Tube site where Beth and her friends had posted videos for Ms. Werner. Each segment started with a childhood picture of the woman speaking. They hadn't exactly been ugly ducklings, but they certainly had resembled chicks who having lost their down, had not fledged out their adult feathers yet. All grown up, they gave a very different impression.

"My name is Gladys Garvey Crandel, I'm President and CEO of Port Langly Construction. We employ 206 people and have an annual operating budget of $84 million. I am the voice of Calliope Jane."

"Hello, Ms. Werner, I'm Sarah Smith, formerly Sarah Nohles. One day when I was seven, you were ahead of us in the check-out line at Woolworths. I was fascinated with the pinwheels, but my mother couldn't afford toys. You bought a pinwheel and handed it to me, telling me to follow my dreams. Today, I study wind energy at your alma mater, when you're feeling better, I hope you'll come visit. We're making great strides reducing our country's dependency on fossil fuel and foreign oil. What I do makes a difference: I am the voice of Calliope Jane."

"Sister Mary Frances Coogan here, director of Mother of Mercies Orphanages in Rio de Janeiro. I oversee two facilities that house and protect 110 children. These are some of the girls who graduated from our program that takes children off the streets and gives them new lives."

The camera panned back to reveal a group of cheerful young women who smiled broadly and shouted: "Bonita ou simples, use seu cerebro! Eu sou a voz de Calliope Jane!" Translation: Pretty or plain, use your brain. I am the voice of Calliope Jane!

There were several more videos, and Ms. Werner watched in silence, occasionally wiping her eyes with the corner of the bed sheet. At the end, she reached over and took hold of Beth's hand. "What a silly old fool I've been, lying here feeling sorry for myself, thinking my life was an insignificant waste because I hadn't been a star. I had no idea."

"No, I'm sorry," Beth apologized. "I should have told you what you meant to us years ago."

Ms. Werner waved her hand dismissingly. "Wouldn't have mattered. I wasn't in the mood to hear it. All I could see was that *my* dreams hadn't come true. It wasn't until this illness brought me to a standstill that I started talking *to* God instead of *at* Him. I spent most of my life being bitter, not any more. Could we watch it again?"

They watched the videos a second time with Beth adding more details to help Ms. Werner connect faces with places. They laughed, and they cried.

"That was wonderful, just wonderful!" nodded Ms. Werner with a sniff. "Hand me some more tissues, and please, don't leave without showing me how to find it again."

"It's here, my daughter set up a link for you, and she's coming over to put it in your icons. Oh, here she is now. Ms. Werner, this is my daughter, Penny. Penny, this is Penelope Werner, the lady you're named after."

The pleasant woman stepped to the bed and gave Ms. Werner a warm hug that surprised and pleased the older lady. "I'm so glad to meet you. I've heard about you all my life. I wish I could have heard your show."

"You can," laughed Ms. Werner. "When Fred sold the radio station, I asked for them, and he sent me the tapes. I had them copied onto cds. If you have time to go get them, there's a set in my apartment next door. I bought the building several years ago when my folks were still alive."

"The building next door," repeated Beth. "Penelope Werner, Penner Holdings, why didn't I make that connection?" she wondered out loud.

Ms. Werner chuckled. "Were you the agent on that deal? How funny! I kept telling my business manager I felt like I was negotiating with myself." She dug in her purse and handed her namesake a ring of keys adding: "The cds are in the bookcase, and my Bible is a couple of shelves up, would you, please, bring it too? Now that I have my head on straighter, I'd like to get reacquainted with an old friend."

# HARVEST GOLD AND AVOCADO GREEN
―――❦―――

We sat side-by-side on the step by the curb, I couldn't bear to say goodbye. We'd been together for 24 years, how do you just let go of that? I held on the way you cling to the hand of a terminally ill friend and thought:

"This is dumb! It's a vacuum sweeper, a worn out vacuum sweeper. Stop carrying on like you're losing your best friend."

Easier said than done though. I remembered the day I bought the sweeper. Fresh out of high school and settling into my first apartment, I'd saved my money and done my research, then walked four miles to Sears and purchased a sleek little canister vac. This was not my parents' 1930's black mechanical Bissell sweeper, nor was it their 1950's Buck Rogers style Electrolux with sled runners and a burgundy hose. It wasn't even their 1960's Filter Queen that came with an arsenal of tools and its very own plastic upholstered storage trunk. This was 1970's, space age technology in Harvest Gold and Avocado Green, compact, powerful, and sporty.

The four mile walk back to the apartment was the first of our many moves together. The sweeper was always the last thing loaded into the car, and the first thing taken out at the new place. It journeyed with me through good times and bad, right and wrong, marriages and divorces. It never judged, never criticized, never said: "You threw it, you clean it up."

I pulled the canister closer and ran my hand over the molded plastic housing feeling for a particular dent. Oh man, did I feel like a monster the first time I lost my grip and let the little sweeper tumble down a flight of stairs! But nothing broke, and life went on.

Remnants of crayon embedded in the logo stirred warm thoughts of my son as a toddler. Barely big enough to walk, he would lay across the canister, and I'd pull him around. That's probably why the hose had so much duct tape holding it together, but no amount of duct tape could dull those happy memories.

As I reminisced, I wondered how I had arrived at this place. Not how you wind up with an old vacuum sweeper, things wear out. The question was: how had I become *so* emotionally attached to a household appliance. Was my life so pitiful that things meant more to me than people? Let's see, 24 years with a sweeper was three times longer than any of my romantic relationships had lasted. Yikes!

I examined my life and realized that my house was clean, but my heart was full of crud. I never let go of anything. I hung on to every perceived offense, every hurt feeling, every angry outburst, every loss. They were like trophies on the mantle of my heart, and they were not dusty. Oh no! I kept my misery polished by constantly dwelling on it, and I fed the fire of my grievances by reliving the events, and reminding myself how I had been misused.

Of course, in my mind's eye, I was always the victim. I never started anything, it was never my fault, and I never, no *never*, responded in anger or fought dirty. Yeah...

As the truth emerged, it dawned on me that I gave the appliances I purchased more serious consideration than the relationships I pursued. Emotions always led me, and I had not saved anything that really mattered for someone who really counted.

More than that, I always expected God to forgive my failings, but I didn't want to hear that I should forgive the people who hurt me. Others should be long suffering, but I shouldn't have to guard my temper. And I expected a life-time warranty from the world, when God is the only one who will truly *never leave you or forsake you.*

I had some cleaning to do, and I began laying aside the malice in my heart. I stopped lying to myself, and discovered that the truth might sting, but it wasn't as painful as I expected it to be.

## The Just and the Unjust Alike

"I forgive you," was a sentence I disliked, and I really hated: "Please forgive me." But after choking and gagging and having to spit a few times, I began to speak the words, and discovered that apologizing for my part in disagreements set me free, whether the other person accepted my apology or not!

And as I gave more thought to the words coming out of my mouth, confrontations became the exception not the rule.

One-by-one, as God showed me the emotional trophies I had turned into idols, things I thought about more than I thought about Him, I let go and filled the space with words from the Bible. When you have the Truth, you don't need trophies.

And that *life time warranty* that I wanted, I discovered that it had been mine all along, waiting for me in the blood that Jesus shed on the cross.

1 Corinthians 1:18 *"For the message of the cross is foolishness to those who are perishing, but to us who are being saved it is the power of God."*

# THE GHOST OF JERRY PAGANELLI

❦

"Shut up. Shut up, damn you! SHUT UP!"

"I can't shut up, Bobby, I've been dead for fifteen years, four months, and three days. You know that."

"I know, I know," he conceded. "Gino, gimme another shot!"

"You've had enough, Bobby. Why don't you go home now? You're starting to talk to yourself again, and it makes the other customers uncomfortable."

"If you don't want my business, you jackass, why don't you just say so?"

"I *don't* want your business," bluntly replied the bartender in a low, firm voice. "You're a loud-mouthed drunk and a big pain in the ass. The only reason I put up with you is because your old man was a friend of mine. Now you take this lasagna for your mom, and shove off."

"To hell with you," Bobby spat back. "To hell with all of you! I'll take my business somewhere else."

"Yeah, well good luck with that. Hey! Lasagna." The wobbly drunk ungraciously snatched the plastic bag off of the bar and slammed out, rudely barging his way past an incoming customer.

"What's his problem?" demanded the newcomer.

"He drinks too much," answered the bartender as he went to get the man's carry out order.

An old man at the end of the bar was more talkative. "Been like that for years, nobody knows why. Says he drinks to drown out the voice in his head, but when he gets drunk, seems like that voice bothers him even more. Lives with his mother, she's a nutcase too. Wouldn't let him off the apron strings when he was little. Then his old man died, and she got crazy afraid she'd lose her boy too. Doesn't leave her house anymore."

Meanwhile, Bobby was staggering down the street with the plastic bag swinging from his arm. The foam food container in it squeaked, and the rustling plastic irritated him. He stopped beside a trash can intending to rid himself of the nuisance, but the bag had twisted around his wrist, and he couldn't figure out how to get his hand out.

"If you throw that away, your mom will be upset."

Bobby whipped around wildly tearing at the plastic bag. "Shut up! You're driving me crazy! SHUT UP!"

"I'm dead, and you drive yourself crazy. Don't spill the lasagna."

At the house, Bobby jabbed his key at the lock on the kitchen door several times before hitting the cylinder. Then he had to push hard to force open a wedge wide enough to squeeze through. Something he had to do, what was it? He should take the trash out. Yeah, that's what he should do. What? Oh, yeah, he should take the trash out. Tomorrow, he would take the trash out, tomorrow.

"Bobby...Bobby, is that you?" demanded a small, shrill voice.

"Yeah, Ma, it's me," he answered rubbing his temple in an effort to marshal his thoughts before facing his mother.

"You're so late, I was worried. Would you like to sit down and talk for a while?" she asked doubtfully.

"Not tonight, Ma. I'm tired."

"Okay, well, did you bring me any supper? You know I get hungry around five o'clock."

*"You're not hungry,"* he thought. *"You haven't been hungry in years. You don't do enough to get hungry. You just like to make me feel bad if I don't come home when you want me to."*

Out loud he murmured: "Lasagna," and stumbled over a stack of washed foam carry out boxes as he handed her the food.

"Be careful, sweetheart! Maybe somebody could use those," she suggested.

"Who, Ma? People in Bangladesh live better than we do."

"Nonsense, we live just fine. Would you hand me a fork, please? Not that one, I'm saving it for good, the other one, please."

He obediently handed her a plastic fork with one tine missing and walked away. Stepping over the latest stack of neatly tied newspapers, he half-climbed, half-crawled up the narrow path on the stairs to the second floor.

His bedroom smelled like sweaty linen and stale beer, but in stark contrast to the overcrowded rooms below, it was nearly empty, and what was there looked like something out of a child's room from 25 years ago. A single bed covered by rumpled cartoon character sheets, a chest-of-drawers with one drawer tilted in, and a maple desk without a chair were all that stood on the bare hardwood floor. There used to be a chair, yeah, there used to be a chair. What happened to the chair? Oh, yeah, he threw it out the window.

There were no books, no dusty trophies or faded ribbons, just an old television that connected to the outside world by a cable line snaked through the broken window. Duct tape held a scrap of plywood and what was left of the shattered glass in place, and a faded blanket nailed to the wall served for a curtain.

"Home-sweet-home," he sneered sarcastically as he stretched out on the bed and fell asleep.

Sometime in the night, Bobby woke up with a throbbing head and a dry mouth. He went to the tiny bathroom off of his bedroom to get a drink of water and smacked his head on the slopped ceiling when he forgot to duck.

"Son-of-a-ahh!" He filled a plastic glass with water and carried it to the bed. The water was tepid, and he wished for the millionth time that there was enough room in the refrigerator for an ice cube tray. Just one, he would like to be able to make just one tray of ice cubes, so a guy could have a cold drink of water once-in-a-while.

"If you didn't drink so much, your head wouldn't hurt."

"Shut up."

He wanted to wet a wash cloth to put on his forehead, and when he couldn't find one, he dug in a drawer for a sock and wet it instead. He turned his pillow over, putting the cool side up, and fell across the bed pressing the wet sock over his eyes. Yuck, it smelled like a wet sock. It didn't matter though, his head hurt too much for him to think about anything except making the pain stop.

"You forgot to pick up the laundry."

"Shut up," he repeated tiredly and groped on the desk for the remote. Noise, noise would drown out the voice. The television popped and came to life in the middle of some hokey televangelist program. Bobby began to surf. You have to surf. If you stay on one channel too long, the voice can talk over the television, so you surf.

Free television is worth everything you pay for it. Bobby stole cable service from the man who lived behind him, and he wished to hell that Stan would get something besides Angel Network. Sports, old movies, how about a little porn, would it kill you? He wished for anything in place of the endless stream of rah-rah, happy, sunshine crap that streamed through the cable. Bobby was a pretty squeamish guy, but he thought that anything CSI would be less nauseating than the Hallmark channel. Aspirin, why hadn't he remembered to get aspirin?

He slept for a while and woke up feeling a little better. Still thirsty, he leaned up on one elbow and took several long swigs of room-temperature water.

"Is your life a mess?"

"Aw, shut up!" he exploded before realizing that it was the television not the voice in his head.

"My life was a mess. I was hooked on drugs and alcohol, couldn't get enough sex, and stole anything I could get my hands on to support my addictions. I was mean and angry. I didn't care who I hurt, or who got hurt by what I did. I was such a mess that I decided to end my life."

Bobby glanced at the closet, and thought about the loaded handgun hidden in a shoebox on the top shelf.

"Why don't you? Why don't you just blow your brains out and get it over with?" asked the voice.

"Because it would make a mess for somebody else to clean up, and I've already made enough messes in my life," he replied digging his thumb into the volume control.

The man on the television was saying something that Bobby did *not* want to hear: "Then I gave my life to Jesus and asked Him to be my lord and savior."

Bobby changed the channel. The same program was playing, only running a few seconds behind, so he heard the man say again: "Then I gave my life to Jesus and asked Him to be my lord and savior."

"Go to hell," snarled Bobby swinging his legs over the side of the bed and holding his head in his hands.

"I used to watch shows like this and yell at the screen, telling whoever was talking to go to hell," said the speaker. "But the person in hell, was me. If you've had enough of the life you're living and want things to change, simply ask Jesus to come into your life and be your Savior. Do it right now, just ask."

The speaker went on talking, but the mixed up man on the bed had stopped listening. He *was* sick of his life, and the hell he was living. It had to change. God knows he'd tried on his own and failed, failed miserably. What did he have to lose by asking Jesus to help?

If Jesus knew what he had done, would He help?

The man on the television said: "You might be thinking that God won't forgive you for the things you've done. Well, He forgave Paul for hunting down Christians and killing them, Acts 9; and He forgave Peter for denying Him three times, Luke 22:57-58. Jesus said in John 3:16 *'For God so loved the world that he gave his only begotten son, that whoever believes in Him should not perish but have everlasting life.'* Jesus came to set the captives free, Luke 4:18. You can be set free, right now, just ask Jesus to set you free."

Bobby had nothing to lose, nothing but pain and struggle. "Jesus, the nuns taught us about you, but I don't know you, I don't know if you're real. I'm hoping though, hoping that what this guy says is true. Are You big enough to forgive a no-good, rotten, rat-bastard like me? Would you be that lord and savior for me?"

The man on the television was saying something about healing touch: "If you need healing in your body or in you mind, take a step of faith and lay your hands on the television screen. We're believing in God for a miracle, right now, right this minute."

A power stronger than his self-hatred moved Bobby to the television; he knelt in front of it, and put his hands on the screen. His shoulders slumped as he listened to the evangelist and prayed with him: "Jesus, please, come into my life and save me, please." A warm soothing presence spread through his body, and Bobby felt like he was floating. Maybe he'd died, and this peace was death.

Daylight was peeping through the gaps in the tape on the window when he woke up on the floor, and Bobby knew he was not dead. His head was pounding, and nausea made it difficult to swallow, but something was missing. He lay quietly for a few minutes and waited. No, it wasn't there, the voice that had haunted him for years was gone. In its place was something else, resolve.

He took a shower and shaved, then brushed his teeth and went downstairs. In the kitchen, he picked up as many bags of trash as he could carry and took them to the dumpster in the alley behind the house. It was the first of many trips. By the time his mother got up, he had cleared a path through the kitchen wide enough for two people to walk past each other, without one of them having to lean backwards limbo style.

The refrigerator door stood open. It was empty except for a pan of hot water wedged into the ice-caked freezer.

"Are you going to work today?" his mother asked cautiously.

"Not today, Ma."

"What are doing?" she asked wringing her hands.

"I want some ice."

Her son turned around, and she vaulted from anxious to terrified. "Bobby! What are you up to?"

"I'm gonna go talk to Sully."

"No!" commanded his mother shaking her head at him. "No, Bobby, they'll take you away from me. You go talk to the priest instead. Please, Bobby, please!" she pleaded clinging to his arm.

"What's he gonna do, Ma? Tell me to say the Rosary a thousand times," he countered with weary patience. "I gotta do it. I can't keep living this way." Fear gripped her, but something about him had changed. Her son was calm, and the sense of peace around him had its effect on her.

"I'll call you after I talk to Sully, and when I come home, I'll take care of the rest of the trash. Maybe you could make some ice and clean up a little, while I'm gone."

His mother bit her lips in a self-silencing gesture, and he gently pulled his arm out of her grasp. He really did love her and didn't want to hurt his mother, so he hugged her shoulders and kissed her on the cheek.

"It's gonna be okay, Ma. You'll see."

Half-an-hour later, he entered the Fifth Precinct and asked for Detective Timothy Sullivan. The desk sergeant buzzed him in, and he went to the second floor landing where Sully was waiting.

"What is it this time, Bobby? Assault and battery, disturbing the peace, drunk and disorderly?"

"Murder," replied his godson.

"Jesus, Mary, and Joseph, Bobby! What the hell have you been up to? Not here, go into my office," he ordered glancing around as he roughly propelled the unwelcome visitor down the hallway.

Sully filled two cups with coffee then sat down and rubbed one ham-like hand over his eyes for a

## The Ghost of Jerry Paganelli

minute. Then he covered his mouth and stared across the desk preparing himself for what was to come.

"Okay, give me the details."

"You remember Jerry Paganelli?"

"Yeah, slow kid, used to ride an old bicycle all over the neighborhood and pick up aluminum cans. Committed suicide."

Bobby flinched. "He didn't commit suicide."

"Never tell me you killed him, I wouldn't believe you, Bobby. You used to stick up for him, wouldn't let the other kids pick on the poor guy. What have you got to do with his death?"

"I didn't kill Jerry, I killed me. It was fifteen years, four months, and four days ago, not long after my old man died. I was walking home after the bars closed, and it was raining so hard you could barely see. I was on that narrow bridge over the flood canal, and lightning was flashing all over the place. It was scary as hell, and on the other side of the street, here comes Jerry riding that stupid old bike of his in middle of an electrical storm. Well, Super Hero Bobby to the rescue, I was gonna go take him home, but I was so smashed that I stepped off the curb right in front of a delivery truck. He swerved to miss me, and I could see the driver's face. He was looking at me. He didn't see Jerry. When the truck was out of the way, Jerry was gone, and the bike was laying cock-eyed against the guardrail. I ran across the street and started to jump in, but somebody was already in the water. I didn't see where he came from, but he had his arm around Jerry helping him stand up."

Sully shook his head. "Couldn't have been. The water gets ten feet deep there any time it rains. If somebody had been with Jerry, there would have been two bodies in the spill basin. You were drunk."

"I don't care, I know what I saw. Somebody was helping him."

"Did you go to the funeral?"

"No, I went on a bender."

"Drink your coffee, I gotta get something."

Sully returned carrying a yellowed folder. He flipped it open and turned the file around. Bobby swallowed the lump in his throat and looked at the photo stapled to the jacket. It was Jerry, but he didn't look dead, he looked like a sleeping angel. In place of the tense, scared rabbit expression of someone who got hassled all the time, there was peace. Bobby stared hard at the picture wishing he could communicate with the dead man. "I'm sorry, Jerry, I'll make it right for you, I promise."

"He don't need your help any more, Bobby. You were his friend when it mattered, that's what counts."

Bobby shook his head refusing to compromise. "I have to make this right."

"Yeah," agreed Sully grudgingly, "I suppose you do, but you gotta do it for yourself."

Second on his list of people to see that day was the parish priest. Father Bernard thought he had heard it all, until Bobby told him why he was there.

"My son, are you worried that Jerry went to hell?"

"No way, Father. Jerry wasn't smart, but he was good, always talking to me about Jesus and living right. He didn't go to hell, I did."

"This is very serious, I'll have to consult the Cardinal to see what can be done."

"I already know the right thing to do. There'll be a court hearing to change the official cause of death, and the judge will issue a corrected death certificate. Then Jerry gets moved to the sanctified side of the cemetery, where he should have been all along. I'll pay all the expenses."

It took time and patience to convince the flustered priest that there was a workable solution. Oddly though, the most challenging part of their conversation came when Father Bernard suggested that they have a drink. Bobby shuddered at the thought and excused himself, saying that he had two more stops to make before going home.

Gino's lips tightened into a disapproving line when he saw Bobby come through the door. He leaned into the bar with his hands clenching the drink rail. The wide spread of his arms gave the impression that he was protecting the bottles of alcohol behind him. But for the first time in his drinking career, Bobby wondered whether Gino was protecting the booze from him or, if maybe, his dad's old friend was trying to protect him from the booze.

"Don't even ask," instructed Gino.

"I'm not staying. I just came to tell you, I'm sorry. I've been acting like a jerk for a long time, and you deserve better. You've been a good friend, and I never appreciated you. Thanks for everything: putting up with me, feeding Ma, but most of all, thanks for all the times you told me to go home. You were right."

"What's up with you?" demanded the old bartender suspiciously.

"I guess you could say: I saw the light."

Gino gave him a curious look. "You want to have a cup of coffee and tell me about it?"

"Not today, thanks anyway. Soon though, right now, I got stuff to do," and the most obnoxious customer Gino had ever dealt with held the door for an incoming couple and politely tipped his baseball cap to the lady.

"Thank you, Jesus!" murmured Gino smiling widely. "God does answer my prayers."

Bobby walked one block past his own street and rang the doorbell of the house that sat across the alley from his. His neighbor was surprised to see him, and welcomed Bobby more warmly than he knew he deserved.

"I've come to apologize..." he began.

"Come in, come in, you look like you could use something to drink." Bobby quivered, but his neighbor offered: "Gatorade or Coke?"

"Oh, yeah, Gatorade would be great," Bobby replied taking off his cap and hanging it on the halltree as he passed.

They went to the kitchen, and Stan handed him a bottle of Gatorade and a glass of ice.

Bobby turned the glass and heaved a contented sigh as the ice clinked. He poured some Gatorade and bluntly asked: "How did you know?"

"Takes one to know one. I used to look like that when I was sobering up. How long you been dry?"

"About sixteen hours."

"It gets easier. The shakes go away in a couple of weeks, and you start to feel so good, you never want to go back. What made you stop?"

"I couldn't take it any more. It was either kill myself or get things straightened out."

Although the older man didn't ask any questions, his look of genuine concern loosened Bobby's tongue, and the story spilled out.

"That's a heavy burden to carry. What're you going to do now?"

"Clean the junk out of our house, and pray to God that they don't send me to jail."

"They won't," assured his neighbor. "The jails are too full to worry about you. It's going to go hard with you in the parish though, a lot of people still remember Jerry."

"I know, but I have to make it right. Jerry was my friend, and I let him down." A tear ran down Bobby's face, and he rubbed his cheek against his shoulder. "Oh, and I need to apologize for stealing cable from you."

Stan chuckled: "I know, I've been paying the cable company for you to have service."

"Why didn't you bust me?"

"Who am I to bust you? When my wife died, I was so angry, I pissed off everybody for blocks. I didn't think you'd listen to me trying to tell you that you needed to straighten up your act, but I wanted you to have a chance. So I made sure you had the opportunity to hear good stuff."

Bobby laughed for the first time in a long time. "I used to swear at you for not getting anything but preacher channels; now, I'm glad. I listen to the TV all night…"

"To drown out the voices?"

Bobby took a deep breath. "To drown out my own voice. I beat myself up all of the time, told myself I was dead. Not any more," and he told his neighbor about his experiences the night before.

Stan moved a magnet on his refrigerator and handed Bobby the flier it had been holding.

"I think you'll like this. I go to this group, Celebrate Recovery. We can go together if you want. I'm retired, so any time works for me."

Bobby knew there was strength in numbers and made plans to go to a meeting. They talked a little more then Stan let him out the back gate, so he didn't have to walk all the way around the block to get home.

Bobby opened the door to his own back porch expecting to enjoy the result of his efforts earlier in the day. Finding the porch filled with bags again was discouraging, until it occurred to him that anything on the porch was no longer in the house. Now all he had to do was convince his mother to get rid of the rest of the junk she was hording.

When he opened the kitchen door, the change took his breath away. The path he had started had widened and been scrubbed clean. The counter tops were clear, one side of the sink had soapy water in it, and a dish drainer full of clean dishes occupied the other side. The faint scent of Pine-sol reminded him of happier times, and his mother stood by the refrigerator holding a tray of ice cubes.

He had called her, so she wouldn't worry. He was not prepared for the change freedom from fear made in her.

"Ma, you made ice," was all he could think to say.

"Of course I did, sweetie. It's the only thing you've asked me to do in a long time."

He put his hands over hers and stared into her pretty brown eyes as the revelation of what he had done landed on him. When his father died, Gino and Sully had told him to take care of his mother, and that is exactly what he had done. He had taken care of her to the point that he had crippled her. He never asked his mom for anything or expected anything of her. He had denied her the pleasure of helping herself and her son. On top of that, he blamed her for the mess in the house. Now his words came back to him: *"Tomorrow, I'll take the trash out tomorrow."*

"Ma, I'm sorry! You tell me what you want to keep, and I'll get rid of the rest of this stuff."

"I don't want any of it," she replied. The stupefied look on his face encouraged her to continue. "When your dad died, it was so sudden, there was no time to prepare, he was just gone. I was so upset that I let everything slide. Then about the time I started to feel like I could cope again, you turned angry, and I was afraid to annoy you about the chores. Most of the time, you'd eventually take out one bag of trash, so I separated the recycle stuff from the garbage and washed it.

"If I was braver, I would have taken the trash out myself, but, Bobby, I'm so scared. I'm scared of everything: gangs, terrorist, drive-by shootings, strangers. Strangers are the worst. That awful man attacked Mrs. Colletti, and I haven't had the courage to go outside without you ever since," she trailed off biting her lip.

"Oh my God, is that why you stopped cooking? You were afraid to walk to the grocers?"

"That's part of it. It started after the funeral. People brought us so much food that I didn't know what to do with all of it. I was afraid it would hurt their feelings if we didn't eat it, but neither of us was hungry, and it seemed like such a waste. I froze as much as I could, and we ate that for a long time. Then I got sick and things piled up even more, and the basement got so full that it was hard to get to the washing machine, and you started taking the laundry to Mrs. Kim. Things just kept piling on, and I didn't know how to change direction. After a while, I sort of got used to the clutter and felt safer. With all of this stuff, nobody could sneak up on me."

Bobby set the ice cube tray on the countertop and hugged her.

"Let's get all of this junk out of here and get a security system."

"Can we afford it?" she asked doubtfully.

"Yeah, Ma, we can afford it," he assured her.

"Are you sure? I mean, when your dad died, everyone said that we would probably lose the house. That's what happened when my father died. I'm so afraid we'll be homeless," she confessed burying her face in his shirt.

The specter of her past fears melted his heart even more, and he held her tight: "Ma, do you understand anything about your finances?"

"No," she admitted shaking her head, "your father was the clever one."

"After supper, we're gonna sit down and talk about money. You're not rich, but Dad left you enough to be comfortable, and I make good money too. There's no reason for you to worry."

"Really, oh, that would be so nice!" she sighed. "But, Bobby, you don't always have a lot of work, and I worry that you spend too much on utilities and taxes, taking care of me."

Bobby laughed. "I work enough, Ma. I'm a mean drunk and a major pain in the...neck, but I'm good at what I do, and I get paid very well. We'll be fine. After that, I've got something else I want to tell you about."

"Could you tell me the other thing first? I mean, if it's what made you feel better, I'd like to hear that part first."

The next day, Stan saw them cleaning and volunteered to haul the recyclables to the drop center. Then he helped Bobby move the furniture and clean the rugs. By evening, the house was clutter-free, and it was Rosemary and Stan, instead of Mrs. Bertonelli and Mr. Stanwick. Rosemary walked from room to room, and was amazed. "Without all that stuff, the room seems so big. I feel like a mouse in the Trivoli Palace Ballroom."

"The Trivoli? Rosemary, do you dance?" asked Stan.

"I used to," she replied wistfully.

When Bobby returned from the grocery store, he found them doing the Lindy in the middle of the living room and smiled.

A few weeks later, they were all together again, and Rosemary whispered: "This is silly."

"You don't have to do it if you don't want to, Ma."

"I mean, it's silly for you to stand here with me."

"You sure?" She nodded yes and gently pushed him toward a chair.

"Hello, my name is Rosemary, and I'm codependent. I was afraid of everything until my son got to know Jesus in a way I didn't understand. Bobby told me about God's love, and the freedom that comes from knowing Him, and I got saved too. It's very nice on this side of knowing God."

"Way to go, Rosemary!" someone shouted, and Rosemary breathed in the Breath of Life and laughed joyfully, as the group applauded and welcomed her.

# Extenuating Circumstances

Some conversations are harder to have than others, and I've often wondered why it's easier for some of us to talk to our families about sex than it is to tell them about our salvation.

My oldest sister was a real trooper, one of those people who met adversity head on and didn't flinch. She moaned and groaned a lot, and said: "Good grief!" more times than I can count, but she didn't let life get her down. So when she called one night and asked me to come over because the flu was kicking her butt, I knew something was really wrong. After ten minutes with her, I called her nearest son and the paramedics.

It was January, and two inches of sleet covered the ground turning the ride to the hospital into a slick mess. The ambulance was about five minutes ahead of me, and as I struggled to find the hospital, I slid

## Extenuating Circumstances

through an intersection. The red light camera flashed in my face, and I was furious. "Extenuating circumstances," I yelled. "I have extenuating circumstances here. They'd better not send me a ticket!" I also said some other things that I'll leave out.

A few hours later, tests revealed that my sister didn't have the flu, she had a perforated ulcer that had leaked into her abdominal cavity causing major damage to her organs. They took her into surgery at 2:30 in the morning. I don't know much about medicine, but I know you don't have surgery at 2:30 a.m., unless it's really serious. It was the beginning of the end.

Over the next 39 days, as my intrepid sister lived out the end of her journey, we cried and prayed, and laughed and prayed, and argued and prayed...and prayed. It was so hard. Microscopic moments of hope were followed but gigantic disappointments, and there never seemed to be any relief from the pain that racked her. I knew I'd be devastated when she died, but I was okay with her leaving. It was her suffering that was unbearable.

I went to the hospital every day, and every day, I scowled at the red light camera that had flashed me and growled: "Extenuating Circumstances!"

It was a busy intersection, and I saw several other cars run the same light. But running that light isn't the only traffic violation I saw on the streets around the hospital. In their panic and distraction, people

## The Just and the Unjust Alike

did a lot of crazy things. They made illegal u-turns, drove across the grass, went the wrong direction on one-way streets, drove in the wrong lane on two-way streets, etc, etc, etc.

In the early days, I was so focused on my own cares, that their mistakes exacerbated my stress. Then one afternoon, a young woman changed my perspective. She was leaving as I was arriving, and pulled out right in front of me. She didn't hear the horn blaring or the tires screeching, she didn't even notice that I was inches from T-boning her. She just drove.

Her jaundiced skin was as yellow as her tinted hair, and by the look on her face, I knew she'd just found out that her life was over. There was no denial in her eyes, and I don't think she was surprised, she just didn't know how to process the information. That look broke my heart. And in that instant, I knew things about her you can't possibly know unless God downloads them to you. Primarily, I knew that she had family, but that she was still alone because she didn't have anybody to pray for her, and I began to intercede.

I asked God the Father to forgive her sins and draw her near to Jesus. I asked Jesus to be pour out His love and mercy over her, so she would have salvation. And I asked the Holy Spirit to come along side her with comfort and peace so she wouldn't feel alone. I also prayed that God would heal her any way possible. And, most of all, I prayed for God's will to be done, because He knows best.

My eyes were opened, and through the rest of the 39 days and nights at the hospital, I looked for people in need, and prayed. I prayed for the patients and their families. I prayed for the hospital staff and their families. I prayed for strength and healing. I prayed for reconciliation and restoration in relationships. I prayed for miracles when it seemed that there was no hope. I prayed for understanding when people were not going to live. I prayed that every one around me *would not perish, but have everlasting life.*

The traffic ticket came, and I just paid it; and when people around me drove crazy, I didn't over react, because you see, I have extenuating circumstances. My sister and I had talked. I knew that when she let out her last breath, she was going to Heaven. We had talked, and I knew that Jesus was the Lord and Savior of her life, and I have peace and comfort in knowing that I'll see her again someday.

What does your family know about you?

# Bible References

These are the verses that came to my mind as I wrote. Some may not be exact quotes, but they were the basis for the plot.

**Duty**
To visit widows and orphans—James 1:27
Greater is He who is in you—1 John 4:4
Strengthened herself in the Lord—1 Samuel 30:6
Rock—1 Corinthians 10:4
Let your light shine—Matthew 5:16
Trust in the Lord—Proverbs 3:5-6
A soft word turns away wrath—Proverbs 15:1

**Mrs. Murphy and the Mob**
Can do all things—Philippians 4:13
Served in his own sauce—Matthew 7:2
Carried like a shield—Ephesians 6:16
His mercy endures—Psalm 118:29
Then He spoke a parable—Luke 18:1-8

**Bubba's Girl**
That I may open my mouth boldly—Ephesians 6:19

**Not Yet**
You have persevered—Revelations 2:3-4
Stars only God—Psalm 147:4
Restore unto me—Psalm 51:12

**Somebody's Daddy**

**Calliope Jane**
Transfigured—Mark 9:2-6

**Harvest Gold and Avocado Green**
Never leave you or forsake—Deuteronomy 31:6 and Hebrews 13:5
Lay aside malice—1 Peter 2:1
Whoever guards his tongue—Proverbs 21:33
Truth shall set you free—John 8:32
For the message—1 Corinthians 1:18

**The Ghost of Jerry Paganelli**
Free indeed--John 8:36

**Extenuating Circumstances**
Forgive her sins--Mark 2:1-9
Draw near to Jesus--John 6:44
Mercy, peace and love--Jude 1:2
Comfort of the Holy Spirit--Acts 9:31
Pray for healing--James 5:16
Not my will, but God's will--Matthew 26:39
Open eyes--Acts 26:18
Would not perish--John 3:16

CPSIA information can be obtained at www.ICGtesting.com
Printed in the USA
LVOW13s2100070714

393258LV00006B/18/P